AV-8 Harrier

Written by Joe Michaels Ph.D.

Cover Paintings and Profiles
Don Greer

Illustrations
Ike Anderson

Color Series

(Front Cover) A Harrier AV-8B II Plus from Marine Attack Squadron (VMA)-223 supports Marine ground troops in Al Anbar Province, Iraq, in late 2005. Flares are being discharged from the ALE-39 flare/chaff dispensers located in the ventral aft end of the aircraft. This system is designed to protect the aircraft from heat-seeking missiles. Four additional ALE-39 dispensers are positioned on each side of the heat exchanger ram air intake directly forward of the vertical stabilizer.

(Back Cover) A VMA-211 AV-8BII (NA), BuNo.164545, lands aboard USS *Tarawa* (LHA 1) on 9 June 2005 during the 13th Marine Expeditionary Unit's Special Operations Capable Exercise (SOCEX) in preparation for a deployment to the Western Pacific.

(Preceding Page) A brace of AV-8B (NA)s from section one of VMA-513 "Nightmares" flies over the mountainous terrain of Afghanistan sometime during the squadron's 2005 deployment. Both aircraft are carrying two 300-gallon fuel tanks. A GBU-12 is located on station three under the port wing of the lead aircraft, and a LITENING pod is located on station five under the starboard wing *(T. Moore)*

ISBN 978-0-89747-545-7

If you have any photos of aircraft, armor, soldiers, or ships of any nation, particularly wartime snapshots, why not share them with us and help make Squadron/Signal's books all the more interesting and complete in the future? Any photograph sent to us will be copied and the original returned. The donor will be fully credited for any photos used. Please send them to:

Squadron/Signal Publications
1115 Crowley Drive
Carrollton, TX 75006-1312 U.S.A.
www.SquadronSignalPublications.com

About the In Action Series

"In Action" books, despite the title of the genre, are books tracing the development of a single type of aircraft, armored vehicle, or ship from prototype to the final production variant. Experimental or "one-off" variants can also be included. Our first "In Action" book was printed in 1971.

Acknowledgements

Lockheed Martin (LM)
McDonnell Douglas
S. Bottaro
T. Chee
C. Donath
R. Fortunato
J. Kent (LM)
M. Krassort
D. Linn
R. Marchant
S. Miller
M. Roth
K. Shagman (LM)
W. Stolze
I. Turniano
S. Watson
T. Ziengenthaler

Dedication

This book is dedicated to all the gallant Marines who serve worldwide to protect our freedom, and who strive to help freedom-loving people throughout the world. This book is especially dedicated to three Marines very dear to me — an uncle, a brother-in-law, and a son — who served their country, respectively, in World War II (Guadalcanal), post-Korea, and post-Viet Nam. *Semper Fi.* (*Semper Fidelis*, a Latin phrase meaning "Always Faithful," was adopted by the U.S. Marine Corps as its motto in 1883.)

An AV-8B II Plus from Marine Medium Helicopter Squadron (HMM)-262 (ET tail code) settles gently to the deck on 21 January 2006. HMM-262 (Reinforced) is serving as Aviation Command Element with the 31st Marine Expeditionary Unit (MEU).

Foreword

This is the second Harrier in Action book published by Squadron/Signal Publications. My good friend Don Linn authored the first edition in 1982. Many significant upgrades have been made to this remarkable aircraft that include engine upgrades, structural changes, new avionics, and new weapons. In addition, the Harrier is now flown by the Indian Navy, the Italian Navy, and the Royal Thai Navy. The major emphasis of this book will be devoted to the latest versions of the Harrier and the new air arms that operate the Harrier.

Although the U.S. Marine Corps is scheduled to retire its Harriers in 2012 when the F-35 enters service, it is expected that Harriers will still be operating with foreign air arms of the world for a number of years beyond 2012.

Introduction

When Leonardo da Vinci envisioned a vehicle that could vertically take off and land, and then made a sketch of his concept, the stage was set for one of man's most ambitious and challenging adventures. In our industrial world of today, the use of the words "concept aircraft" are taken to mean a new design that has tremendous potential. It is also understood that this will require highly motivated industrious designers, and an army of skilled people to transform a mental image into a flying machine that warrants the investment of time, energy, and capital.

Once Orville and Wilbur Wright made their successful flight at Kitty Hawk, North Carolina, the enthusiasm for flight exploded. But it was not until 1935 that serious consideration was directed toward vertical/short takeoff and landing (V/STOL). Two French engineers, Louis Breguet and René Dorant, designed a coaxial rotor helicopter that flew. In 1939 the Russian engineer Igor Sikorsky, who had emigrated from Russia to the United States, succeeded in developing a single rotor-type helicopter that attracted attention to the concept of V/STOL.

Military minds throughout the industrial world began to explore new ways to gain an advantage on the battlefield. Germany in World War II produced the Bachem BA-349-A1 "Natter," a vertical launch aircraft that was loaded with two dozen unguided 73 mm rockets that were to be fired at the waves of bombers that were attacking Germany. Once the rockets were fired, the pilot was to bail out. The aircraft was to descend to the ground with parachutes attached. Only one flight was made and resulted in the death of the test pilot and the loss of the aircraft.

A variety of V/STOL concepts were investigated during the 1930s, '40s, '50s, and '60s with lift engines embedded in the wings or fuselage like the Mirage III V, Short SC.1, Dassault Balzac, Ryan X-13, Lockheed XFV-1, Convair XFY-1, and the Bell X-14. All of these aircraft had serious drawbacks but contributed significantly to the development of the Harrier.

In 1953, the V/STOL concept was being studied in the form of the Rolls-Royce Thrust Measuring Rig. It had two Rolls-Royce Nene turbojets that were installed horizontally at opposite ends of the assembly and became known as the "Flying Bedstead." Although this platform was incapable of flight, it provided guidance on puffer and autostabilization requirements.

This invention with a pilot sitting on top of two Nene engines was known as the "Flying Bedstead." It was produced by Rolls-Royce and referred to as the Rolls-Royce Thrust Measuring Rig (TMR). It is seen hovering at Hucknall Aerodrome in 1955 in Nottinghamshire, England. The "Flying Bedstead" was used to test the principles of jet-powered vertical flight. Two were built. *(BAE Systems)*

In 1956, Michel Wibault, an aviation visionary and aircraft designer, had a proposal for a combat aircraft that he named the "Gyropter." His invention, in which a gas turbine drove four large centrifugal compressors through gearboxes and shafts, was revolutionary. The genius of Wibault produced an apparatus that delivered a lift force that passed through the aircraft center of gravity (CG). He also concluded that if an aircraft were to hover, a condition in which ordinary control surfaces are useless, it would require an extra control system using reaction control valves (RCVs) on the wingtips, tail, and ventral nose area that would be fed by compressed air.

Wibault's concept, coupled with brilliant engineers like Stanley Hooker, Theodore von Karman, Charles Marchant, Gordon Lewis, Pierre Young, and Neville Quinn, led to a series of engine designs. The Bristol Orion turbojet engine resulted in the Orpheus engine, which led to the BE.52. In the normal course of design refinements, the BE.52 became the BE.53, and then the BE.53/2. This engine — the heart of the Harrier — was redesignated Pegasus (in Greek mythology, a horse with wings).

(Clockwise from upper left)

The Short SC.1 was a slow aircraft that weighed approximately 6,620 pounds. It had four vertically mounted RB.108 lift engines and one RB.108 engine in the rear that provided thrust for forward flight. The SC.1 was equipped with the first "fly by wire" control system for a vertical takeoff and landing (VTOL) aircraft. Two SC.1s were built — XG900 and XG905. *(BAE Systems)*

On 29 April 1964, James F. "Skeets" Coleman, a lieutenant colonel in the Marine Corps Reserve and a Convair test pilot, made the first tethered flight in the Convair XFY-1 "Pogo." In 1973, the aircraft was transferred to the National Air and Space Museum in Washington, D.C. *(Convair)*

The XFV-1 housed a turboprop engine that drove a pair of 16-foot contra-rotating propellers. The pilot sat on a gimbal-mounted seat that allowed 45 degrees of swivel. The XFV-1 was named the "Salmon" after the chief engineering test pilot Herman "Fish" Salmon. Two prototypes were ordered under the designation XFO.1. *(Lockheed)*

Developments

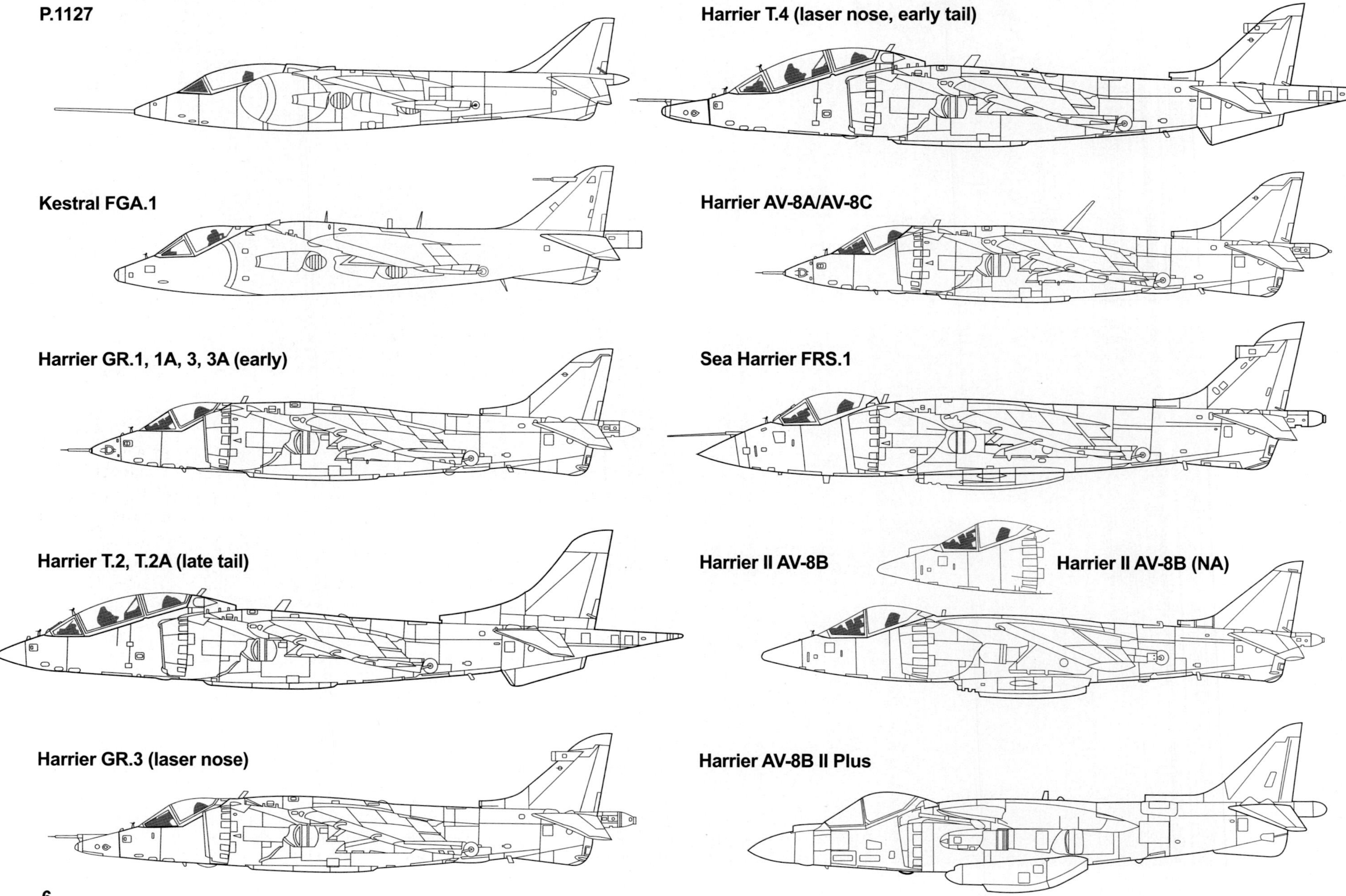

The first Kestrel soars above the English countryside in March 1964 with Tripartite Evaluation Squadron (TES) roundels on the upper surfaces of both wings. The aircraft was in natural metal, but the lips of the intakes were black rubber. *(HSA via D. Linn.)*

Hawker P.1127 XP980 sits broadside at RAF Biggin Hill in September 1966. The aircraft introduced the anhedral tailplane (horizontal tail surfaces of an airplane including the stabilizer and the elevator) and streamwise wingtip fairings. Taxiing trials and undercarriage load measurement tests were conducted at RAF Gaydon in 1972 and 1973. Its first flight was in May 1963. *(Iain Macpherson via S. Miller)*

P.1127

In March 1957 Ralph Hooper, a young British engineer working for the Hawker Siddeley Aircraft Co. in Kingston, England, had prepared a three-view drawing of a project designated P.1127. It was apparent that this particular aircraft design offered very little with regard to payload, range, or speed. The design might have been ignored were it not for the fact that Hawker needed a long-term project. Other projects were not progressing, such as the P.1121, which was to be a Mach 2 successor to the very successful Hawker Hunter, and the P.1129, a twin-engine, two-seat aircraft designed to meet the TSR-2 requirements. Both projects were not mustering the support needed to make them viable.

Central to the success of this radical design was the powerplant. The world's first jet lift cruise engine evolved from the Orpheus turbojet engine, an engine that offered a vectored thrust of about 8,000 pounds. In the summer of 1957, a new machine with four-poster jet lift (four columns of thrust to fly vertically) was a reality. The project engineers were able to modify the ratio of flow through the front and rear nozzles to achieve an increase of an additional 1,000 pounds of thrust.

This engine was known as the BE.53/2 engine. The P.1127 was designed around this engine, which became known as the Pegasus 1. The rear jet was split in two (as on the Hawker Sea Hawk) and exhausted through a second pair of rotatable nozzles in the fuselage sides. By the summer of 1960, two P.1127s were produced in Kingston. Serial numbers XP831 and XP836 were allocated. On 13 March 1961, test pilot Bill Bedford made the first approved flight. The second prototype XP836 made its test flight on 7 July 1961 using conventional takeoff and landing (CTOL). This aircraft was lost on 14 December 1961 when the port engine nozzle came off in the air. Bedford, the test pilot, attempted to land at Yeovilton, but when he lowered the flaps the aircraft went into a roll that could not be arrested, and he was forced to eject.

In November 1960, four more P.1127s were funded by the Ministry of Supply and were designated as "development aircraft." They were XP972, XP976, XP980, and XP984. The first of the development batch (DB), XP972, crashed at Tangmere on 30 October 1962. The last three DB aircraft, XP976, XP980, and XP984, later received the Pegasus 3 engine, which had 13,500 pounds of thrust.

The P.1127 was methodically modified. The fifth P.1127 received a kinked wing leading edge that increased the chord at the tips. A row of 11 upper surface vortex generators on each wing to prevent wing drop at high Mach numbers was added. Improved outrigger gears without pointed-nose fairings, Kuchemann streamwise wingtips, a modified tailplane with a greater area, and an anhedral (near zero dihedral) of 18 degrees were some additional modifications. Improved reaction control valves (RCVs) were installed, and for a limited time inflatable rubber inlet lips were in use. These lips could be inflated to a large radius for hovering and deflated to give a sharp lip for high-speed flight.

Kestrel

The evolution of the P.1127 to the Kestrel was significant because of the installation of the Pegasus 5 engine, which had 15,500 pounds of thrust. The engineering team at Bristol had fitted the high-pressure turbine with air-cooled blades, and this enabled the gas temperature to increase from 977 degrees C to 1,177 degrees C. This boost in power enabled the P.1127 to carry a small war load and more fuel.

Larry Levy

The P.1127 up to this point could only be considered a basic research machine, and the program may have died were it not for Larry Levy, an affluent American who had joined the Mutual Weapons Development Program (MWDP) headquartered in Paris in late 1959. Levy was able to influence his American, British, and German colleagues to fund a Tripartite Evaluation Squadron (TES). The Kestrel, in addition to having the Pegasus 5 engine, also had a new swept wing with a thicker center section, which resulted in a hump in the fuselage.

The aircraft with the new wing was first flown on XP984, which was the final P.1127. The first Kestrel XS688 FGA.1 (fighter, ground attack) flew on 7 March 1964, soon after the last P.1127 had rolled out of the factory in Kingston. This aircraft was more Kestrel than P.1127. All the surviving P.1127s by this time had been significantly modified from the original design. The Kestrel had the pitot head on the fin instead of a long nose probe, and a forward oblique camera was installed in the nose. The tailplane had a pronounced anhedral and a wider span to improve longitudinal stability. The fuselage was lengthened, the air intakes were revised, and the engine was repositioned. Two wing hard points, each able to carry a 100-gallon fuel tank, were installed. A small gun sight was fitted to allow tracking evaluation.

The TES received the last P.1127 as well as the nine Kestrels and was formally set up at Dunsfold on 15 October 1964. Its commanding officer was Wing Commander D. Mcl. Scrimgeour, RAF. The developmental and evaluation aircraft had the serials XS688–XS696. The Tripartite Evaluation Squadron moved to RAF West Raynham, Norfolk, following training and began operational evaluation in April 1965.

TES Composition

The TES was composed of pilots and ground personnel of the RAF, U.S. Air Force, U.S. Navy, U.S. Army, and the German Luftwaffe. Surprisingly, no U.S. Marine personnel were part of this squadron. Its assigned mission was to study V/STOL and all its ramifications. Approximately 600 hours were flown in 938 missions in the program, which was completed in November 1965. The squadron lost one Kestrel (SX691), which crashed on 1 April 1965.

Of the nine aircraft assigned to the TES (XS688–XS696), six aircraft were shipped to the United States and were primarily used as research aircraft. NASA at Dryden and Langley did some interesting research, but the required 50-hour overhaul on each engine was a restricting factor.

NASA 521 was one of two XV-6A Kestrels that were transferred to the NASA Langley Research Center. NASA received two Kestrels, namely, N520NA and N521NA. N521NA was used in air combat maneuvering, where it utilized thrust vectoring in mock combat with a NASA T-38A Talon. The XV-6A Kestrel is suspended from the ceiling at the Virginia Air & Space Center located in Hampton, Virginia.

The fifth Kestrel, FGA Mk1 XS695, first flew on 17 February 1965. During one of its test flights, it crashed at Aeroplane and Armament Experimental Establishment (A&AEE), Boscombe Down. It was repaired and later delivered to the Royal Aircraft Establishment (RAE), Farnborough. The aircraft was photographed at this site in September 1969. *(Jean Magendie via S. Miller)*

British Harrier GR.1

The cancellation of the P.1154, which was to be a multirole combat aircraft with jet V/STOL capability, in February 1965 by the British government resulted in the government giving the green light for Hawker Aircraft to study the smaller subsonic P.1127 as a potential tactical aircraft for the RAF. However, there was the belief amongst many British engineers that cancellation of the P.1154, a project that would have made England the first country in the world to place a supersonic V/STOL fighter in service, was a terrible mistake.

The P.1154 program, under the direction of John Fozard, encountered the same problem the Americans were trying to address with the F-111 — commonality. The RAF supported the P.1154 program, but Her Majesty's Government (HMG) dictated that the P.1154 should fulfill Royal Navy needs for a Sea Vixen replacement. The leadership at Kingston made every effort to address the commonality factor. Extensive redesign and consideration of a twin Spey powerplant resulted in a two-year delay. Cost overruns and time sounded the death knell for the program.

Even the P.1154 program was coming to an end. The government instructed the leadership at the Hawker Aircraft Co. to modify the Kestrel to house the 19,000-pound version of the Pegasus, fit the avionics systems that were being developed for the P.1154 (minus the radar), change the aircraft to increase the weapons load, and deliver an attack fighter to the RAF within five years. After a 90 percent redesign of the Kestrel, the Harrier entered service with the RAF on April 1969 with the formation of the first operational squadron in the RAF. No. 1 Squadron was based at RAF Wittering, home of the Operation Conversion Unit (OCU).

A total of 78 GR.1 models were produced and equipped five RAF squadrons, No. 233 OCU, and Nos. 1, 3, 4, and 20 Squadrons. The first production aircraft were XV738–762, XV776–810, and XW916–924. All these Harriers had the Pegasus 6 Mk 101 engine rated at 19,000 pounds of thrust. The Pegasus 6 Mk 101 engine had an all-titanium fan, two stages of cooled turbine, a revised combustion system with water injection to maintain thrust to higher temperatures, a revised fuel system, and two vane nozzles. The life of the engine was increased to 300 hours.

The first production GR.1 XV738 flew on 28 December 1967 and was piloted by Duncan Simpson.

Strake, Aden 30 mm Gun Pod

Strake

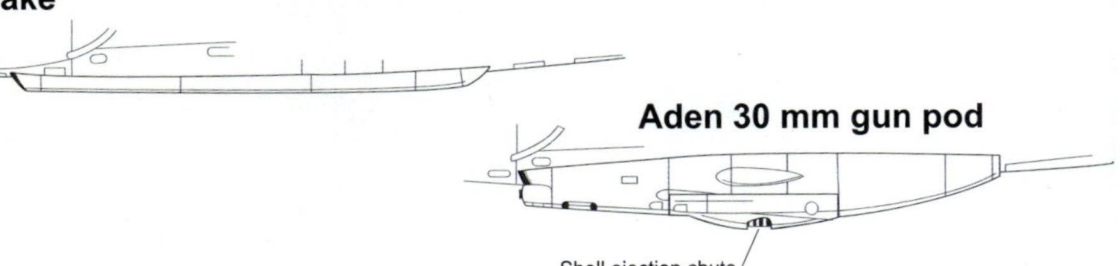

Hawker Siddeley Aviation Ltd. (HSA) retained GR.1 XV742 for trials and training. At one point in time, it was painted in U.S. Marine Corps markings for demonstration purposes. This aircraft appeared at the Farnborough International Air Show on 11 September 1970 with rocket launch pods on the outboard pylons. The "WF" tail code is usually associated with VMA-513. *(L. Soldeus via S. Miller)*

On 26 March 1970, this GR.1 XV780 had its first flight. It is seen with the forward landing gear chocked, but still attached to a tow tractor. The markings of No. 4 Squadron are located on both sides of the aircraft. The home base for this squadron is RAF Gutersloh, Germany. This Harrier crashed in Germany following a bird strike; the pilot ejected safely.

The first flight of this GR.1 took place on 3 April 1969. This aircraft was delivered to No. 1 (F) Squadron at RAF Wittering on 18 April 1969. It was subsequently assigned to No. 233 Operation Conversion Unit (OCU), RAF Wittering, in December 1973. This aircraft crashed into a mountainside near Tromso, Norway, on 12 March 1976. This photo was taken at Andrews AFB, Maryland, on 17 May 1969. *(S. Miller)*

This GR.1, XW766, was delivered to No. 3 (F) squadron in February 1972. It suffered some damage in October 1972, but it was repaired. It was later converted to a GR.1A. The "A" identified it as a GR.1 with the Pegasus 102 engine that produced 20,500 pounds of thrust. This aircraft was again upgraded to a GR.3. *(H. J. Broekhuizen)*

This GR.1, XV276, took to the air for the first time on 31 August 1966. It was based at HAS Dunsfold from 1966–1973. In June 1971 it made an appearance at the Paris Air Show. The large, white "464" signifies that it was a participant in the show. In October of the same year, the aircraft crashed at Dunsfold, due to the throttle stop being out of adjustment. The engine flamed out, and the pilot ejected safely.

XV278 was one of six P1127s, XV276–XV281, designated GR.1 Developmental Batch (DB). This aircraft was used for trials and other work by BAE, Rolls-Royce A&AEE, RAE, and other operators. It used the Pegasus 6 engine that was rated at 19,000 pounds of thrust. It wears the markings of No. 4 Squadron at RAF Gutersloh in Germany.

British Harrier GR.3, GR.3A

The Harrier GR.3 received the new Pegasus 11 Mk 103 engine and produced a thrust of 21,500 pounds. The increase was the result of a rebladed fan that increased mass flow. The engine received an upgraded fuel system, and the water injection system and the turbine cooling system were improved.

An almost 40 percent increase in thrust means that the GR.3 can accommodate heavier loads, such as fuel and weapons. The aircraft can take drop tanks on the inboard pylons, two outboard pylons, and a fuselage pylon. Two 30 mm Aden gun pods with up to 130 rounds per gun can also be mounted under the center fuselage. These pods also act as strakes to increase the ground cushion effect. A port oblique camera is located in the nose. A five-camera pod with a data conversion unit records longitude, latitude, and aircraft headings on film.

The GR.3 uses the Ferranti FE 541 inertial navigation system that presents the aircraft's position in a large head-down map display in the cockpit. Other equipment includes a VHF and UHF radio, UHF homing, HF radio, tactical air navigation (TACAN), and IFF. Externally, the GR.1, GR.1A, and early GR.3 are basically the same.

The "thimble nose" on the GR.3 distinguishes this model of the Harrier from its predecessors. The Ferranti laser range and marked target seeker (LRMTS) was added to the stock GR.3, as was a radar warning receiver (RWR) with forward-looking fin antennas and aft-looking antennas in the fairing behind the tail pitch control Reaction Control Valves (RCVs). The system is the ARI.18223 by Marconi Space and Defence Systems (MSDS).

During the Falklands War, the GR.3 (laser nose) did not have a modern navigation/attack system; it was still using an analogue system. It did not possess any provision for dispensing chaff or infrared (IR) flares. It did not have any jamming equipment installed, nor did it have a system for air-to-air missiles. The lack of equipment to permit its inertial system to function on a moving deck was another serious deficiency.

GR.3 Noses

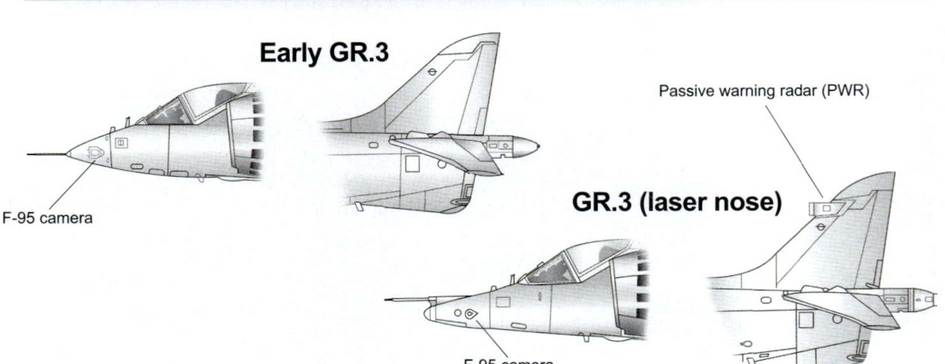

Harrier squadrons have had some outstanding tail colors over the years. This GR.3, XZ969, (laser nose) No. 4 (F) Squadron aircraft was photographed at a base in Italy in the fall of 1990. (See its profile on page 25.) *(S. Bottaro)*

This GR.3 (laser nose) from No. 3 (F) Squadron shows off its white tail at a base in Italy in February 1989. In addition to the serial number XZ995, it also carried the black letter "J" above the fin flash. The GR.3s were limited in the amount of ordnance that they could carry. The Matra 155 was the weapon of choice; when its load of 2.68-inch rockets was fired, the effect was quite spectacular. *(L. Storti)*

British Harrier GR.5, 5A

The Harrier GR.5 is very similar to the Boeing AV-8B. In 1986, the Ministry of Defense (MOD) formally approved the purchase of 60 Harrier GR.5s. Forty-one were completed as standard GR.5s, and the final 19 were completed as GR.5As. Two additional aircraft were ordered for developmental work.

Externally the nose had a different shape than the AV-8B. The underside fairing was to house the miniature infrared line scan (MRLS) system, but the project was postponed indefinitely. This system was designed to give the GR.5 all-weather reconnaissance. The GR.5, like the AV-8B, originally had the Litton ASN-130 inertial navigation system (INS) installed, but eventually all the Harrier GR.5s were retrofitted with the Ferranti FIN 1075 system.

The GR.5s have four pylons under each wing, with a pair of AIM-9 Sidewinder launch rail positions in the front of the outrigger wheel fairings, and one fuselage pylon. In place of the AV-8B's GAU-12/U Gatling gun, a pair of Royal Ordnance 25 mm Aden gas-operated revolver-cannons were installed.

The engine selected for the GR.5 was the Pegasus Mk 105 with 21,700 pounds of thrust, which also had the digital engine control system (DECS). This system monitors the performance of the powerplant and manages the propulsion system.

The GR.5 differed also from the AV-8B in having the underwing pylons slightly modified to carry the BL755 cluster bombs that contain 147 bomblets in several bays. The bomb is heavier and has more mass than the Mk 82 iron bomb, which is carried by USMC AV-8Bs. The leading edge of the wing was made thicker, and the intake lips and windscreen were strengthened to withstand a 1-pound bird strike at 690 mph. These strengthening measures were taken because of the low-level high-speed mission assigned to the GR.5. The Harrier GR.5 uses the Martin-Baker Mk 12 ejection seat in place of the Stencels. The cockpit layout is quite different than the AV-8B's cockpit layout.

The initial development aircraft ZD318 first flew on 30 April 1985 at Dunsfold with Mike Snelling as the pilot. Development aircraft (DB2) tested the engine and systems and was used for ordnance trials. The first GR.5 was not delivered until May 1989 due to avionics fit problems and weapon clearances.

The first GR.5 ZD323 arrived at RAF Wittering on 30 April 1987 and was assigned to the GR.5 Conversion Team (GR.5CT). No. 233 Operational Conversion Unit (OCU) became operational in April 1986. No. 1 (F) became fully operational with the GR.5 in November 1989. No. 3 (F) squadron at RAF Gutersloh, Germany, reached operational status in April 1990. The Bascombe Down-based Strike Attack Operational Evaluation Unit (SAOEU) had three GR.5s attached in the early 1990s. GR.5 ZD328 arrived on 26 July 1988.

A GR.5A is basically a GR.5 with an empty GR.7 nose. It is complete with all the wiring for the new systems to be used in the GR.7. Nineteen were produced: ZD430–ZD438 and ZD461–ZD470.

(Above) This GR.5, ZD410 with No. 3 (F) Squadron, has its upper surfaces painted in NATO IRR Green (BS381C:285) and its undersurfaces painted in Medium Green (BS480012.B.25). The squadron colors are carried on the tail band (green with narrow yellow stripes). The specific aircraft identification letter (AF) is black. *(W. Stolze)*

(Below) A GR.5, ZD402 from No.1 (F) Squadron, prepares to launch with a GR.7 from No. 3 (F) Squadron at RAF Gutersloh, Germany, in May 1991. The GR.5 has two 300-gallon fuel tanks on the inboard pylons as well as an inert acquisition round. *(M. Krassort)*

(Below) This GR.5, ZD412 (AH) from No.3 (F) Squadron, experienced a mishap at RAF Gutersloh in Germany on 30 September 1991. It ran off the runway and crashed through a wooden fence, finally coming to rest in a stream called the Ems. The aircraft was retrieved and put back into service following the necessary repairs. *(W. Stolze)*

British Harrier GR.7, GR.7A

The Harrier GR.7, aside from the nose area, looks externally like a GR.5. With regard to capabilities, the GR.7 is far superior to the GR.5. The GR.7 can operate at night and in poor weather conditions. This has been made possible by the addition of a GEC forward looking infrared (FLIR) scanner located on the upper surface of the nose. On the underside of the nose are the external antennas for the Marconi Zeus ECM system, as well as the eye for the angle rate bombing system (ARBS).

The 75 percent leading edge root extension(LERX) that was initially installed on the GR.5s and early GR.7s will be replaced by the 100 percent LERX on the new GR.7s. LERXs are fillets added to the front of the Harrier's wings that provide usable airflow at high angles of attack.—

The first GR.7 to have the 100 percent LERX was ZG506. Since the 100 percent LERX covered the original holes in the area where the LERX was installed, new small air scoops are positioned above the LERX. The Sidewinder launch rails have been refitted with the Swedish-made BOL system, which cuts and fires chaff from a rear dispenser.

The final 35 of the 96 single-seat Harrier IIs built for the RAF were delivered as GR.7s. The remainder were converted by British Aerospace (BAE) from GR.5s and GR.5As. No. 4 Squadron converted straight to GR.7s from the GR.3 (laser nose) on 12 September 1990 with the arrival of ZG473.

Additional improvements for carrier operations included a mounted Garmin 100 GPS receiver that was used in the Sea Harrier, new software improvements to the aircraft's INS to ease alignment on a rolling carrier deck, a new IFF transponder, and a shift of the water replenishment point from the top of the aircraft to inside the undercarriage bay to make it easier and safer for the flight deck crews.

This GR.7, ZG858, taxies with a Sidewinder missile on the missile launch rail and a Sidewinder acquisition pod on the outboard pylon. A wing commander's pennant is positioned on the nose cone. This aircraft is based at Boscombe Down, the home of the Strike Attack Operational Evaluation Unit (SAOEU). *(R. Marchant)*

The pilot of this GR.7, ZG857, does a last-minute check of his instruments as he awaits takeoff clearance. The GR.7 made its maiden flight in May 1990, and the aircraft made its first operational deployment in August 1995 over the former Yugoslavia. *(M. Remfert)*

Harrier GR.7 ZD407 from No. 20 (F) Squadron taxies at RAF Fairford in July 2004. This colorful Harrier has only the inboard pylons attached. The aircraft was specially painted for the 2004 air show season. (See its profile on page 27.) *(R. Marchant)*

British Harrier GR.9, GR.9A

The major factor that led to the decision to upgrade the GR.7 to a GR.9 specification was the need to improve the capabilities of the GR.7. The GR.9 variant was under consideration for a number of years, since a determination had been made that it was essential to have a Harrier force standardized in order to improve reliability and maintenance.

When it was decided to establish a unified Harrier force that was to be known as Joint Force Harrier (JFH), a decision was made to retire the FA.2 Sea Harrier and upgrade the GR.7 and 7As to GR.9s and 9As. These upgraded Harriers would then serve with the Royal Air Force and Fleet Air Arm.

Sixty GR.7s are to be upgraded to the GR.9 standard. At the heart of this upgrade is the MIL.STD 1760 stores management system (SMS), along with a new main computer system with modernized weapons software, a new GPS-INS navigation system, a ground proximity warning system, and improved cockpit displays. This integrated weapons program (IWP) unifies a number of weapons systems. Sixteen of the GR.9s are to be fitted for carriage of the thermal imaging airborne laser designator (TIALD) pod. At least 40 GR.7s will have the Pegasus 107 engine installed, and these aircraft will be designated GR.9As.

The improved fire-control system of the GR.9/9As will permit the use of the new Macron Brimstone anti-armor missile, an advanced model of the U.S. Hellfire weapon. There is also the possibility that the GR.9s will be configured to carry the new Storm Shadow cruise missile.

The GR.9/9A has four wing weapon pylons under each wing and one pylon on the ventral side of the fuselage. It can carry conventional or cluster bombs, two Sidewinders, and up to 16 Mk 82 or six Mk 83 bombs. Paveway II, III, and IV guided bombs, CRV-7 rocket pods, and the aforementioned Brimstone missiles and Storm Shadow conventionally armed stand-off missile (CASOM) are all part of this aircraft's lethality.

All remaining GR.7/7As will be brought up to the GR.9/9A standard. This model of the Harrier will equip four operational squadrons and one training squadron. A number of systems on the GR.9/9A will be integrated and linked by a new onboard computer that includes the precision-guided bomb and infrared and television variants of the Maverick missile. The inclusion of the Successor Identification Friend or Foe (SIFF) will reduce the vulnerability of the aircraft in a combat zone.

The first GR.9 Harrier flew at BAE Warton on 30 May 2003.

A GR.9, ZG511 (White 82) assigned to No. 1 (F) Squadron, taxies at RAF Cottesmore in July 2006. To distinguish the GR.9 from the GR.7, the letters GR are in white on the tail with a black 9 superimposed over the letters, positioned between the white 82 and the blue and red marking. The refueling probe is extended on the port side of the aircraft. *(P. Marchant)*

This GR.9, (White 73) ZG502 from 800 Naval Air Station (NAS), visited the Czech International Air Fest in Brno, Czech Republic, in September 2006. It carries the red and yellow chevron on the fin cap and the squadron insignia on the intake fairing. A red protective cap covers the ARBS camera lens on the tip of the nose cone. *(K. Vogler)*

This Harrier GR.9, ZD431 (43A) from 800 NAS, taxies from its home base at RAF Cottesmore in July 2006. The squadron badge is worn on the forward nozzle housing, and the red with yellow border stylized chevron is visible on the fin cap. The Pegasus Mk 107 engine provides approximately 3,000 pounds of extra thrust, significant when operating in hot climates. *(P. Marchant)*

British Harrier T.2, T.2A, T.4, T.4A, T.10, T.12

Ralph Hooper produced the first drawing of what was to become the Harrier T.2. His proposal was to have a tandem-seat cockpit. To accommodate the extra weight, the shift in the center of gravity, and aerodynamic center, a ballasted section was to be added to the tail. The major concern was directed toward increasing the engine thrust needed to lift this heavier airframe into the air. The initial contract for two development batch aircraft was initiated in 1966. A single-seater was modified by moving the cockpit forward 47 inches, and a second cockpit was installed in the original cockpit area, but raised 18 inches. This would enable the nose wheel to be retracted under it, and the forward view would be enhanced.

New canopies that were hinged on the starboard side replaced the single rearward sliding canopy. The air conditioning system was upgraded and positioned aft of the canopy. In addition, the inertial platform and F-95 camera were moved from the nose to a position below the rear cockpit to lessen the problem of balance. The vertical stabilizer was moved 33 inches and placed on an 11-inch stub, and the enlarged ventral fin was installed on the underside of the fuselage centerline. Approximately 170 pounds of ballast was added to the tailcone to maintain the aircraft's center of gravity (CG).

The T.2 was now 450 pounds heavier than the single-seater with reference to basic weight plus pilots. The T.2 has the full navigation-attack system, but the rear cockpit lacks the moving map display.

The first prototype Harrier T.2, XW174, flew on 22 April 1969, and was piloted by Duncan Simpson. It was destroyed on 4 June 1969 due to a fuel system failure. The second aircraft, XW175, flew on 14 July 1969. It was discovered that the aircraft lacked directional stability above 15 degrees angle of attack (AOA). After several engineering changes failed to improve the situation, it was decided to extend the tip of the vertical tail in increments of 6, 18, and 23 inches. A decision was made to go with the 18-inch increment. Because of the directional stability problem inherent with all Harriers, they all land with the airbrakes deployed . At one time there were two standards of fin on the T.2 before all the two-seaters reverted to the GR.1 tail shape.

Two development aircraft (XS174–175) and 12 production T.2s (XW264–272 and XW925–927) were produced with Pegasus 6 Mk 101 engines. However, XW926 and XW-927 were completed as T.2As and had the Pegasus 10 Mk 102 engines.

The Harrier T.4 was the new designation of the T.2/2A after the Pegasus 11 Mk 103 engine was installed. Externally, it could be distinguished from the T.2/2A by the laser ranger and marked target seeker (LRMTS) nose and the ARI 18223 radar warning receivers (RWRs) located on the forward section of the vertical stabilizer and the tail cone.

The Harrier T.4A had the Pegasus 11 Mk 103 engine and RWRs, but did not have the laser nose. One T.4A was funded by the Royal Navy prior to the purchase of the Royal Navy T.4N.

When the RAF's frontline Harrier was the GR.3, the old T.4 trainer was adequate for basic pilot conversion training, even though a new two-seat trainer was available in the shape of the TAV-8B. Plans to upgrade the T.4 to a T.6 to support GR.5 and GR.7 training was abandoned when it was realized that this was not cost-effective in light of the advances that were being projected for the new Harrier variants. The T.10, unlike the USMC TAV-8B, is fully combat capable. Unlike the TAV-8B, which has only two underwing pylons, the T.10 has eight underwing pylons and is FLIR equipped. Two empty gun pods instead of two ventral strakes are always fitted beneath the fuselage of the T.10. This increases longitudinal stability in forward flight.

Fourteen T.10s were produced. The first was built at Dunsfold from components produced at Brough, Kingston, and Wharton in the United Kingdom, and additional components came from St. Louis, Missouri. The first T.10, ZH653, made its maiden flight on 7 April 1994. The first aircraft delivered to the RAF was ZH657 at RAF Wittering on 30 January 1995. The T.10 was introduced to service on 1 March 1995, and the last T.10, ZH665, was delivered to No. 20 Squadron.

The T.12 will have the IWP upgrades necessary for the training of GR.9/9A pilots, and like the earlier marks of the RAF two-seat Harriers, the T.12 will have combat capability.

This T.2 XW175, one of two developmental aircraft, made its first flight on 14 July 1969. In 1971, it made an appearance at the Paris Air Show held at the Le Bourget Airport. All participants were required to have a special number, hence the large white "465" on the starboard fuselage.

This tandem-seat trainer Vectored Thrust Aircraft Advanced Flight Control (VAAC) is based at Boscombe Down. In September 1999, the VAAC Harrier made the first ever fly-by-wire landing onto the deck of the HMS *Illustrious*. *(R. Marchant)*

Harrier T.2 Second Seat Installation

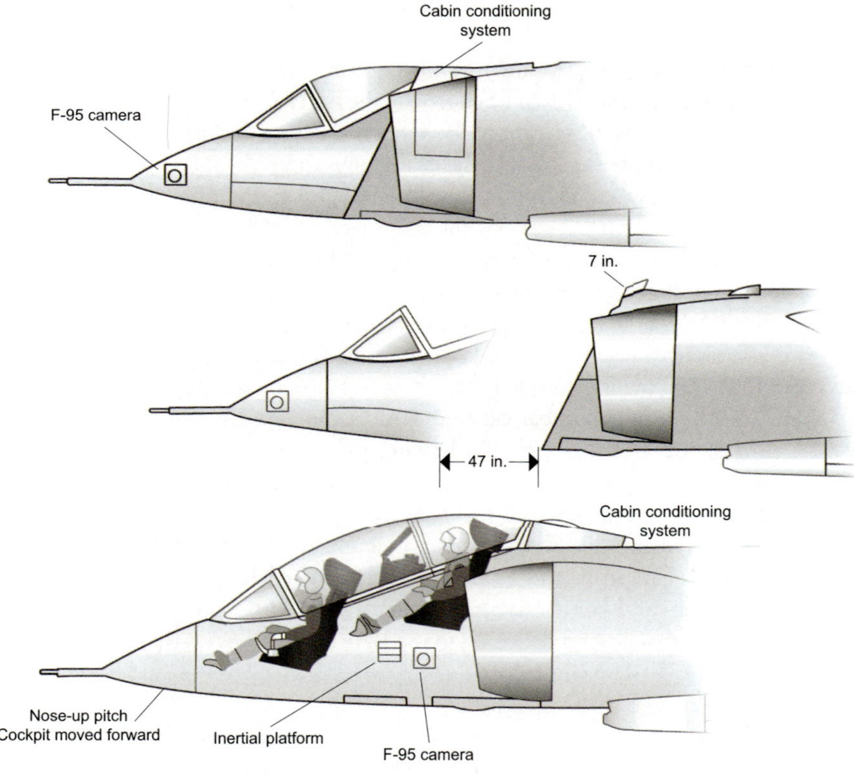

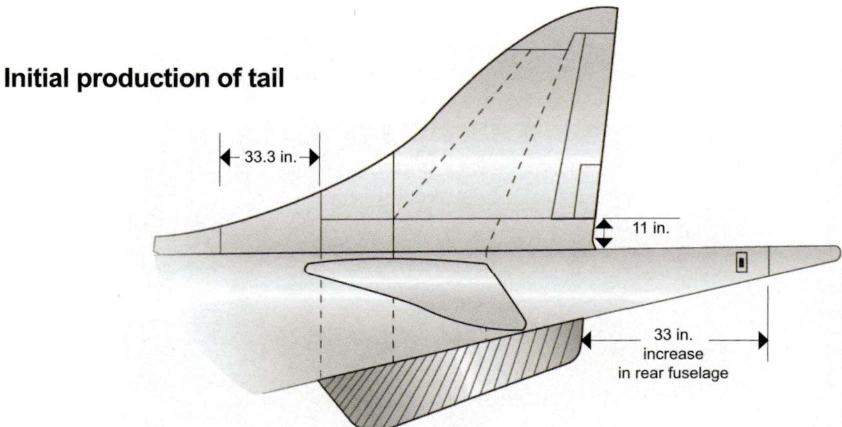

A T.4, XW927 of No. 4 (F) Squadron, makes a straight-in landing at RAF Gutersloh on 15 October 1985. Its first flight was 8 June 1972, and in July 1972 it was assigned to No. 233 OCU. It was originally built as a T.2A with the Pegasus 11 Mk 103 engine and was retrofitted with the laser nose and the radar warning receiver positioned in the vertical stabilizer. *(W. Stolze)*

This T.10, ZH654, belongs to A&AEE Boscombe Down. It made a visit to the Fairford International Air Tattoo (IAT) on 21 July 1995. It was painted overall NATO IRR Green (BS381C:285). *(R. Marchant)*

British Sea Harrier FRS.1

In 1969, The Royal Navy began studying the possibility of a carrier-based variant of the Harrier. It wasn't until 1972 that Hawker Siddeley Aviation (HSA) was awarded a contract to study the idea.

This was to be a minimum change program, but magnesium had to be deleted from the engine components of the engine since salt water might pose a corrosion problem. The magnesium components of the engine and airframe were replaced with aluminum alloys. There was also the need for a forward-looking radar for the air defense role. Ferranti, an Italian-based electronics company, was given the contract to develop the Blue Fox radar. Rolls-Royce was given the contract to develop the Pegasus Mk 104 engine. The cockpit was completely redesigned, and the canopy was bulged to improve visibility over the intakes.

Initially the Royal Navy was to require 24 Sea Harriers, but in 1978 a subsequent order for 10 additional Sea Harriers and four trainers was placed. These new trainers were based on the RAF T.4. Three squadrons were to be established: Nos. 800, 801, and 802. No. 802 Squadron existed only for a few months before it was redesignated No. 809 Squadron.

Externally, the Sea Harrier differs from the RAF Harrier in having a raised cockpit and a radar nose. The floor of the cockpit was raised 10 inches, which improved the rear view over the intakes and provided space for more equipment. The recovery control system (RCS) was improved by installing larger reaction control valves (RCVs); this enabled the aircraft to cope with the turbulence caused by the carrier superstructure. A high-speed autopilot was put in place to ease the workload of the pilot in normal flight, which is most advantageous during a long flight. The inertial platform was replaced by a twin gyro platform and a Decca 72 Doppler radar. A new Smiths head-up display/weapon aiming computer (HUD/WAC) system was installed along with a radar altimeter. The presentation of the radar warning information was improved. The Martin-Baker Mk 10H replaced the Mk 9A ejection seat. In addition, two AIM Sidewinders can be carried on the outboard wing pylons. A 4-inch section was added to the height of the fin to compensate for the RWR addition on the forward section of the vertical stabilizer and the raised cockpit. A small but important modification was adding deck tie-down lugs to the nose gear strut. The first flight of the Sea Harrier, XZ45 piloted by John Farley, was made on 20 August 1978.

Following the Falklands War, the RN Sea Harriers incorporated a reconnaissance data link, an audio AOA system, a speed trim device that will facilitate hover positioning, as well as various armament and radar changes. The cockpit was completely redesigned.

This FRS.1, ZD607 from 899 NAS, has a Sidewinder on its starboard pylon. The ventral brake panel is usually left in the open position when the aircraft is not moving. This Sea Harrier made its first flight 12 August 1985 and was delivered to the Royal Navy on 6 November 1985. It was converted to an FA.2 and eventually was assigned to RAF St. Athan Battle Damage Repair Training (BDRT). *(M. Krassort)*

On 1 May 1982, Lt. Cdr. N. Thomas flew an attack mission on Stanley Airport dropping three 500-pound bombs. On 21 May 1982, Lt. Cdr. M. B. Blissett destroyed an Argentine A-4C with an AIM-L Sidewinder. On 16 March 1984, this Sea Harrier, XZ496, ditched in the North Sea off the Norwegian coast near HMS *Illustrious*. The pilot ejected safely. *(D. Linn)*

This FRS.1, XZ499 of 809 NAS, was aboard the HMS *Invincible* when it visited the Philadelphia Naval Yard in 1985. The name "ETHEL" is written in black on front of the port intake below the canopy. This aircraft had one confirmed kill during the Falklands War. The aircraft at this time was assigned to 800 NAS and flown by Lt. Smith; it is presently stored at RNAS Yeovilton. *(D. Linn)*

An NAS Yeovilton-based Hunter T.8M Blue Fox radar trainer visited Decimomannu, Italy, a primary NATO training base in Sardinia, Italy, in July 1986. All Sea Harrier pilots train on the T.8M. The cockpit was modified by having radar controls installed, giving trainee "Shar" pilots hands-on experience with radar operations. (Sea Harrier FRS.1 was informally known as the "Shar.") *(C. R. Stewart)*

This FRS.1 Sea Harrier, ZA175 from 899 NAS, sports a commemorative paint scheme on the tail celebrating the squadron's 50 years of service. This aircraft was flown by Lt. Cdr. "Sharkey" Ward during the Falklands War, in which he shot down a Mirage V Dagger using an AIM-9L Sidewinder. The aircraft at the time was assigned to 801 NAS. It was later converted to an FA.2. *(R. Marchant)*

FRS.1 XZ450 was a participant in the 1979 Paris Air Show. The oversized white "241" is the identification system used by the French Air Show authorities. This Sea Harrier crashed at Goose Green, Falkland Islands, on 4 May 1982 after being hit by anti-aircraft fire. The pilot, Lt. N. Taylor of 800 NAS, was killed.

An FRS.1 and T.4N from 899 NAS sit untethered at RAF Waddington in the United Kingdom in April 1990. Both aircraft are carrying 190-imperial gallon (864 liter) external fuel tanks. *(M. Krassort)*

British Sea Harrier FA.2

The FA.2 came into being as the FRS.2. This was a logical designation for an aircraft that followed the FRS.1. In reality, it made little sense to use the letter "R" since the Sea Harrier had such a limited range. The "S" for strike was changed to "A" for attack since the nuclear strike mission was not critical after the tactical nuclear forces of the Western World were deemed to be less critical following the breakup of the Soviet Union.

Following the Falklands War, the deficiencies of the FRS.1 were studied, and the end result was that there was an expressed need for a better Sea Harrier. It was recognized that the radar system as well as the weapons system and avionics needed to be upgraded. The range of the aircraft needed to be improved by providing larger wing fuel tanks.

In 1985, British Aerospace was issued a contract for an upgraded Sea Harrier. This laid the groundwork for the production of the FA.2. Piloted by Heinz Frick, aircraft ZA195 had its first flight on 19 September 1988 at Dunsfold. This aircraft was the first modified Sea Harrier prototype (DB1). It lacked the new radar and carried an instrumental pitot static probe in the bulbous nose.

The main upgrades included the new Blue Vixen radar, the ability to carry four AIM-12 advanced medium-range air-to-air missiles (AMRAAMs). The FA.2 is approximately 13.75 inches longer than the FRS.1. The powerplant is the Rolls-Royce Pegasus 106 that is capable of 21,750 pounds of thrust. The FA.2's wing is different from the FSR.1's in that the dogtooth was moved near the wing root to improve air flow at high angles of attack when carrying 190-gallon drop tanks. The middle of the wing has a subtle bend where the midwing dogtooth was located on the FSR.1.

The last FA.2 Sea Harrier built, ZH813, was delivered from Dunsfold to RAF St. Athan on 18 January 1999.

This FA.2, XZ497 from 801 NAS, basks in the sun at RAF Waddington in July 2001. It first flight as an FRS.1 took place on 2 April 1982. This was the first production FA.2 conversion. An Aircraft Maneuvering Instrument (ACMI) is located on the outboard port pylon. *(R. Marchant)*

This special paint scheme commemorates 25 years of Sea Harrier service in the Royal Navy. The aircraft ZH809 from 899 NAS, known affectionately as the "Admiral's Barge," taxies at RAF Fairford in July 2004. The 25 years is in yellow on the tail. The underside is gloss white, and the upper surface is a dark blue. (See its profile on page 27.) *(R. Marchant)*

Martin-Baker Mk 10H Ejection Seat

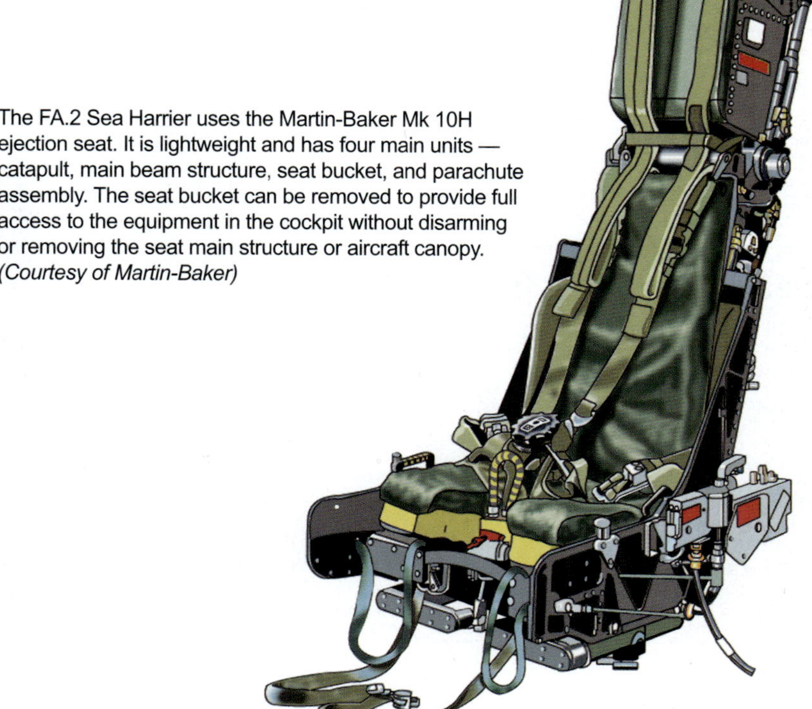

The FA.2 Sea Harrier uses the Martin-Baker Mk 10H ejection seat. It is lightweight and has four main units — catapult, main beam structure, seat bucket, and parachute assembly. The seat bucket can be removed to provide full access to the equipment in the cockpit without disarming or removing the seat main structure or aircraft canopy. *(Courtesy of Martin-Baker)*

Sea Harrier FA.2

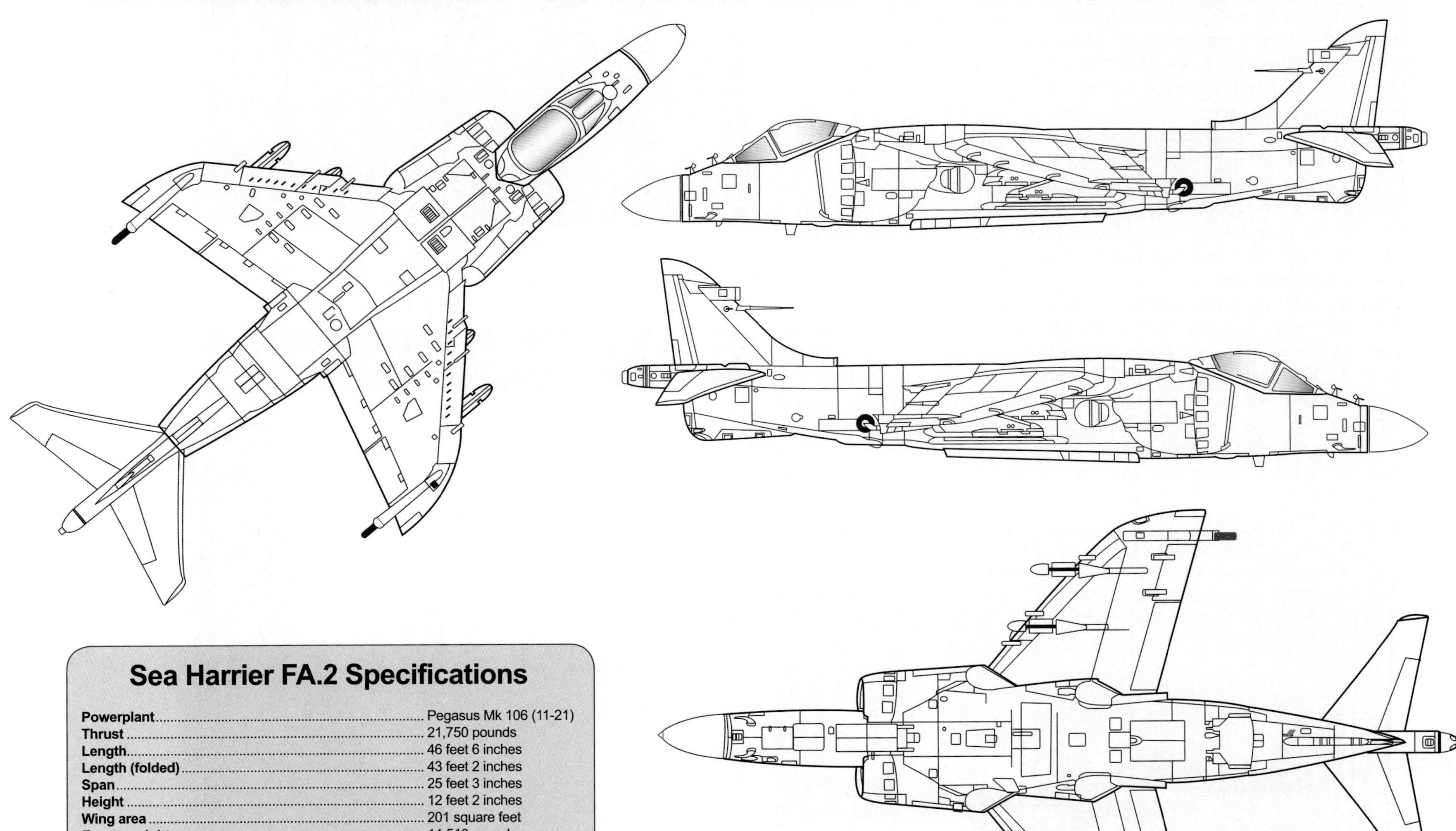

Sea Harrier FA.2 Specifications

Powerplant	Pegasus Mk 106 (11-21)
Thrust	21,750 pounds
Length	46 feet 6 inches
Length (folded)	43 feet 2 inches
Span	25 feet 3 inches
Height	12 feet 2 inches
Wing area	201 square feet
Empty weight	14,510 pounds
Internal fuel	5,060 pounds
Maximum external load	8,500 pounds
Maximum speed at sea level	Mach 0.98 (746 mph)
Combat radius	400 nautical miles
Service ceiling	51,000 feet

This FA.2, ZH803 from 800 NAS "Satans," sits broadside to the sun loaded with a Sidewinder AIM-9L on an LAU-7 launcher shoe on the outboard pylon. A pair of advanced medium-range air-to-air missiles (AMRAAMs) on the LAU-106 launch rails are carried in place of the twin Aden 30 mm gun pods. *(R. Marchant)*

During operations Deliberate Force and Sharp Guard, 800 NAS did not carry squadron tail markings, and the British roundels were Pale Red (RDM28A) and Pale Blue (RDM28A). The normal Dark Red used to delineate critical areas on the aircraft were painted Pale Red. The serial number on this FA.2 is ZH799, and the number 004 located on the forward nozzle is painted white. *(L. Storti)*

An FA.2, ZH813 from 801 NAS, approaches NAS Yeovilton in July 2005. It was the last new-build FA.2 in the batch of 18. The serial is in white located on the tail bumper. The aircraft number 006 is in white. The overall paint scheme is Medium Sea Gray (BS381C:637), but the external 120-gallon fuel tanks are Dark Sea Gray (BS381C:638). *(J. Bosma)*

This FA.2 Sea Harrier, ZD612 from 899 NAS, wears the Medium Sea Gray paint scheme (BS381C:637). The gun pods, starboard outboard pylon, and external fuel tanks are Extra Dark Sea Gray (BS381C:640). The nose cone is a weathered Dark Sea Gray with a black band. The angular flying fist squadron emblem has a Dark Gray outline. *(L. Storti)*

The fifth T.8 upgrade, ZB604, was built as a T.4N and delivered to 899 NAS on 21 May 1983. Since the Royal Navy did not use the laser range and marked target seeker (LRMTS), its aircraft were never modified with the extended nose. (See its profile on page 28.)

British Harrier T.4N, T.8

The T.4N is similar to the Royal Air Force's T.4, but is used for Royal Navy land-based training. Three aircraft were built and delivered to the RN between 1983 and January 1986. The T.4N is combat capable, but it will not fit on the elevators of British carriers; therefore, a T.4N cannot be stowed below deck.

The seven T.8 trainers are all conversions from existing Royal Navy and RAF two-seaters. The T.8 is similar to the T.4N but features updated avionics and a cockpit layout that better matches the Sea Harrier FA.2. However, the T.8 is not fitted with the Blue Vixen radar found on the FA.2. The initial flight of the first T.8 was in 1994, and the first delivery was in 1995.

The T.8 has the Pegasus Mk 106 engine installed, but is not radar equipped. It has the multifunction and head-up display (HUD), and is capable of carrying AIM-9 Sidewinder acquisition rounds.

This tandem seat dual trainer, XW268, was the fifth production aircraft built as a Harrier T.2. It served with the Royal Air Force before being transferred to 899 NAS. It was written off on 27 June 1994. *(M. Krassort)*

T.4N ZB604, assigned to 899 NAS, wears the Dark Sea Gray scheme. It appears that the aircraft has received a new wing or has been recently painted. The wing is painted in Medium Sea Gray (BS381C:837). The wing roundels are Pale Blue and Pale Red, unlike the fuselage roundels that are Post Office Red (BS38lC:538) and Roundel Blue (BS381C:538). *(M. Brand)*

Marine Harrier AV-8A

The Marine Corps' search for tactical airpower that didn't require an airfield began most likely with Gen. Keith McCutcheon, USMC. He sent a team to the Farnborough Air Show in England in September 1968 that included Brig. Gen. Johnson, Col. Tom Miller, and Lt. Col. Bud Baker. Miller and Baker were both test pilots. Based upon the team's evaluation, contract negotiations began in two weeks. The Marine Corps decided upon a procurement of 114 aircraft, but the final number was 102.

The first aircraft were designated AV-8A, with the prefix A indicating "attack" and the V indicating an aircraft with V/STOL capability. The money for the first 12 aircraft came from funds that were to be used for the purchase of the F-4J Phantom, and was taken from the Fiscal Year (FY) 1970 budget. Bureau Numbers (BuNos.) 158384–158395 (12) were purchased in 1970. BuNos. 158694–158711(18) were purchased in 1971, BuNos. 158948–158977 (30) were purchased in 1972, BuNos. 159230–159259 (30) in 1973, and the final batch of AV-8As, 159366–159377 (12), in 1974. All the AV-8As were built in England by Hawker Siddeley at Kingston.

The major new feature of the AV-8A, which went into production in 1970, was the Pegasus 11 engine that had 21,500 pounds of thrust. The first 10 AV-8As were initially delivered with the Pegasus 10 engine that the USMC referred to as the F402-RR-400. Externally, the AV-8A differed from the GR.1 by having a large VHF/FM radio antenna on top of the wing and outer pylons equipped with wiring that enhanced their shoot-down capability. They could carry the AIM-9 Sidewinder air-to-air missile in addition to the ordnance that the GR.1 could carry.

Very few changes were made to the Marine Harriers. A weight-on-wheels sensor was added, new checklist placards were located in the cockpit, and Navy avionics VHF/FM, UHF, and IFF replaced RAF equipment.

The first AV-8A (BuNo.158384) had its maiden flight on 20 November 1970. It was delivered to Marine Attack Squadron (VMA)-513, based at Marine Corps Air Station (MCAS) Yuma, Arizona, in March 1971. AV-8As also served with VMA-231, VMA-542, and VMAT-203, based at MCAS Cherry Point, North Carolina.

VMA-542 AV-8A BuNo.158699 sits on the ramp at MCAS Cherry Point, North Carolina, in May 1978. It is painted in the standard scheme and colors of the early Marine Harriers. It also has the white practice multiple bomb rack (PMBR) and a 300-gallon external fuel tank on the inboard pylon. This aircraft was written off on 22 September 1983.

This AV-8A from VMA-513 hovers at the NAS Norfolk Open House in April 1973. The upper surface was painted Dark Green (FS 14709) and Dark Sea Gray (FS 16173). The undersurface was painted Light Gray (FS 16440). All the markings were in black. *(A. Vandam)*

Ejection Seats

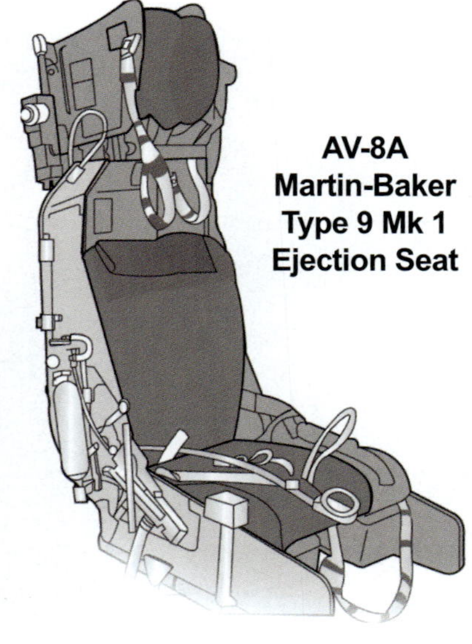

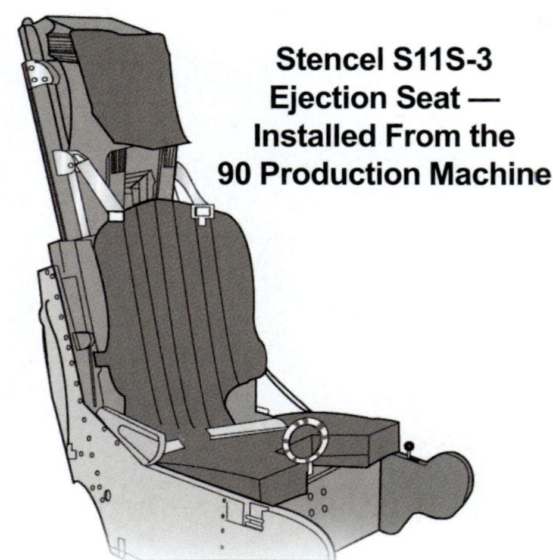

VMAT-203 "Hawks" began receiving their AV-8As in late 1975. This AV-8A (BuNo.159255) wears the same paint scheme associated with the British GR.1. The tail code "KD" as well as the modex 28 is white. The colored stripes on the rudder are red, white, and blue, probably because this photograph was taken at MCAS Cherry Point in July 1976, the month of the United States' Bicentennial.

An intrepid AV-8A Harrier pilot poses in front of his aircraft in the mid-1970s. As of 1980, 39 of the original purchase of 102 had crashed. The line of demarcation between the top colors and the underside of the Harrier is well delineated. Most pilots personalize their helmets by having them painted or by applying colored tape in an eye-catching pattern. *(U.S. Marine Corps)*

An AV-8A from VMA-542 roars past the crowd at NAS Point Mugu, California, in April 1976. The yellow on the tail has suffered the effect of the weather from deployment at sea. VMA-542 was one of the first Harrier squadrons to be established and currently flies the AV-8B Harrier II Plus.

This Harrier sits hidden under a camouflage net at an unknown location. The ability of the Harrier to operate from remote bases or areas difficult to detect makes them a formidable adversary. This early version of the Harrier was approximately 50 mph faster than the AV-8B that replaced it. *(U.S. Marine Corps)*

Harriers in Color

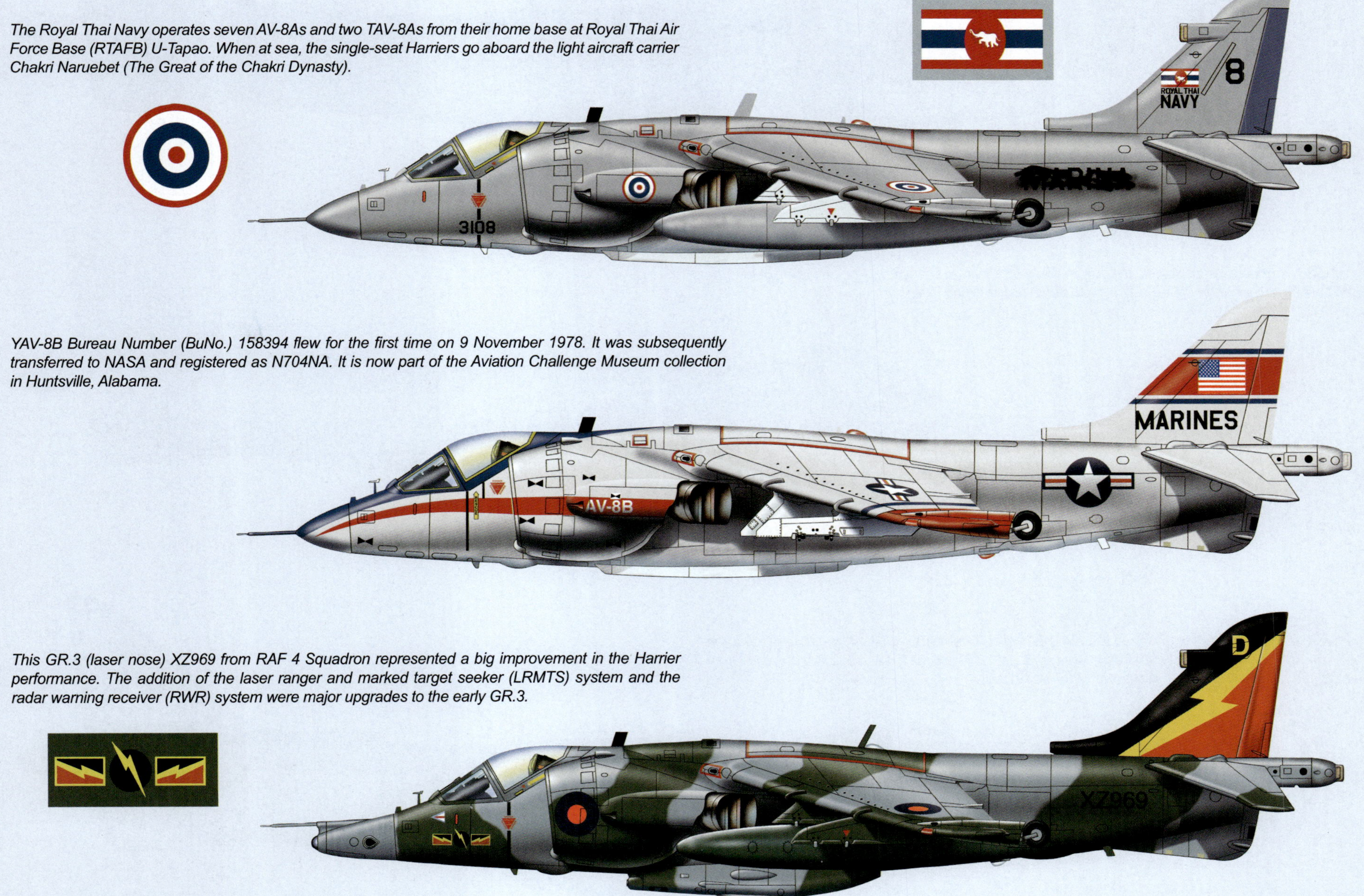

The Royal Thai Navy operates seven AV-8As and two TAV-8As from their home base at Royal Thai Air Force Base (RTAFB) U-Tapao. When at sea, the single-seat Harriers go aboard the light aircraft carrier Chakri Naruebet (The Great of the Chakri Dynasty).

YAV-8B Bureau Number (BuNo.) 158394 flew for the first time on 9 November 1978. It was subsequently transferred to NASA and registered as N704NA. It is now part of the Aviation Challenge Museum collection in Huntsville, Alabama.

This GR.3 (laser nose) XZ969 from RAF 4 Squadron represented a big improvement in the Harrier performance. The addition of the laser ranger and marked target seeker (LRMTS) system and the radar warning receiver (RWR) system were major upgrades to the early GR.3.

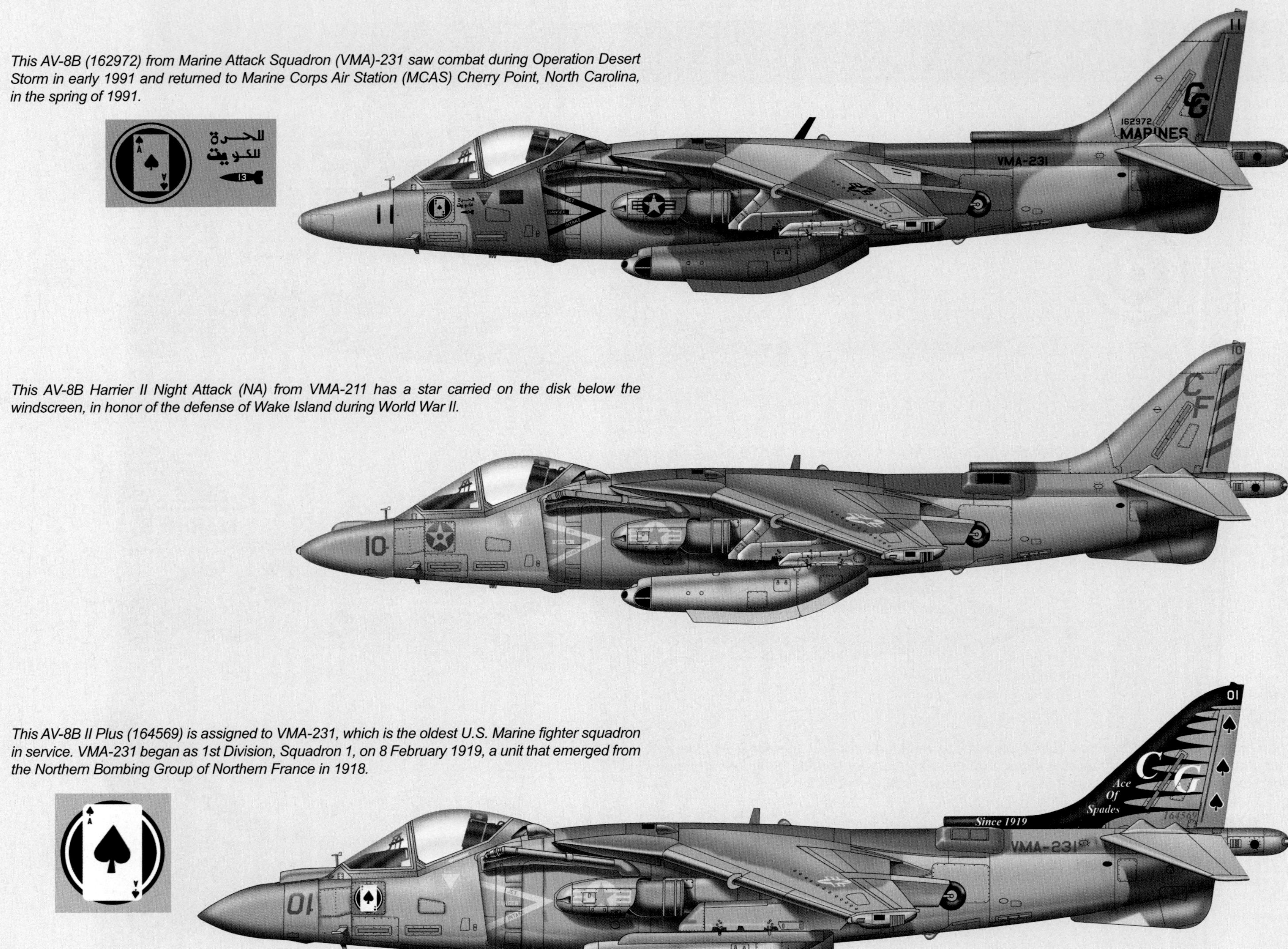

This AV-8B (162972) from Marine Attack Squadron (VMA)-231 saw combat during Operation Desert Storm in early 1991 and returned to Marine Corps Air Station (MCAS) Cherry Point, North Carolina, in the spring of 1991.

This AV-8B Harrier II Night Attack (NA) from VMA-211 has a star carried on the disk below the windscreen, in honor of the defense of Wake Island during World War II.

This AV-8B II Plus (164569) is assigned to VMA-231, which is the oldest U.S. Marine fighter squadron in service. VMA-231 began as 1st Division, Squadron 1, on 8 February 1919, a unit that emerged from the Northern Bombing Group of Northern France in 1918.

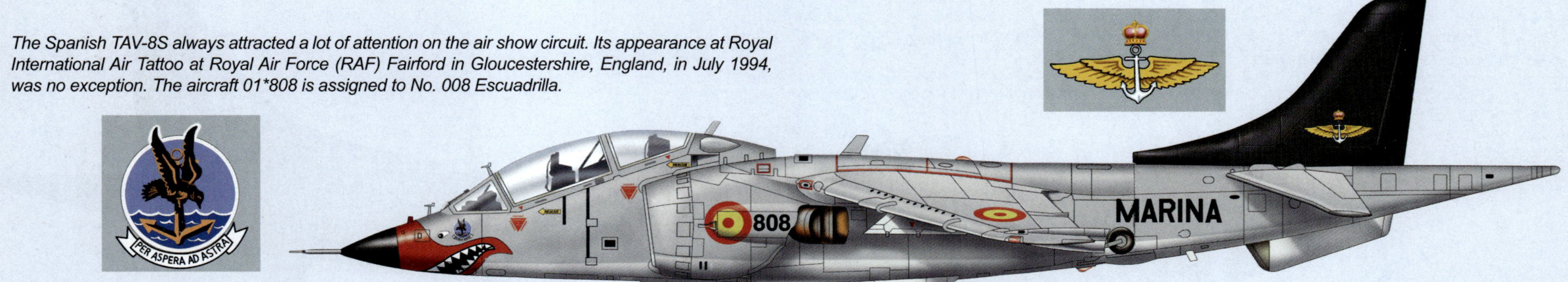

*The Spanish TAV-8S always attracted a lot of attention on the air show circuit. Its appearance at Royal International Air Tattoo at Royal Air Force (RAF) Fairford in Gloucestershire, England, in July 1994, was no exception. The aircraft 01*808 is assigned to No. 008 Escuadrilla.*

This FA.2 Sea Harrier, known as the "Admiral's Barge," is assigned to 899 Naval Air Squadron (NAS). This squadron served aboard HMS Invincible in support of operations in the Adriatic and Bosnia-Herzegovinia during October and November 1993.

This GR.7, ZD407, from 20 (Reserve) Squadron is based at RAF Wittering at Kemble, England. The squadron serves as the Operational Conversion Unit (OCU) for the GR.7. The unit's motto is Verba non Facta (Deeds not Words).

This is a T.8 from 899 NAS. It was built as a T.4N and delivered to 899 NAS on 21 May 1983. The T.8 does not have a radar installed in its nose.

VMA-311 received its first night attack Harrier in May 1992. The assigned squadron tail code is "WL," but when assigned to a Marine Expeditionary Unit (MEU), it adopts that squadron's tail code but retains all markings associated with VMA-311 "Tomcats."

FA.2 Sea Harrier XZ439, the second development aircraft, was detached to Eglin AFB, Florida, in January 1993 for the purpose of conducting live AIM-120 advanced medium-range air-to-air missile (AMRAAM) trials. At the conclusion of the trials, the aircraft was disassembled and flown back to the United Kingdom in an RAF Hercules transport. British Aerospace Dunsfold is written in medium blue.

Marine Harrier AV-8C

Once the U.S. Marines decided the Harrier was the best aircraft to support the Marines on the ground, it became apparent that the next generation Harrier would have to have significant improvements.

While plans were still on the drawing board for the new Harrier, the Marines began working on a major conversion in lieu of procurement (CILOP) program to extend the life of the AV-8As. Important modifications were made to a number of the AV-8As. An airframe overhaul was undertaken to add 4,000 hours to the life of the aircraft; belly lift improvement devices (LIDs) designed for the AV-8B were installed; an updated electronic measures (ECM) suite, including a U.S.-built Litton AN/ALR-45F radar warning receiver with wingtip and tail cone antennas, was installed; strip-style formation-keeping lights were mounted on the vertical stabilizer and forward fuselage; and the side-mounted F-95 camera position in the forward section of the fuselage was deleted.

The upgraded Harriers, AV-8Cs, flew with unconverted AV-8As in four Marine squadrons until the mid-1980s. The AV-8Cs were finally withdrawn from service in February 1987. The AV-8C used the F402-RR-402 engine, which produced 21,500 pounds of thrust.

Approximately 47 surviving AV-8As were upgraded to the new standard. The AV-8Cs retained their AV-8A bureau numbers.

This AV-8C from VMA-513 (WF) is seen coming aboard *Guadalcanal* (LPH 7) on 1 November 1983. One upgrade to the AV-8C was an onboard oxygen generating system (OBOGS). This system enabled the aircraft to generate oxygen for the pilot and eliminated the need to stock oxygen bottles. *(U.S. Marine Corps)*

One visible upgrade to this AV-8C, BuNo.158706 from VMA-542 (WH) "Flying Tigers," was the addition of strip-style formation keeping lights. Another change was the ECM antennas on the wingtips and tail cone. This aircraft sits in front of the squadron's hangar at MCAS Cherry Point.

This YAV-8C, BuNo. 158384, is being towed on the early morning of 8 September 1979 to a display area at NAS Patuxent River, Maryland, where it will participate in the station's open house. Unlike the YAV-8Bs that were converted from AV-8As, this AV-8A did not have the double row of suction intake relief doors. This aircraft crashed on 9 May 1980. *(McDonnell Douglas)*

An upgraded Harrier AV-8C, BuNo.158698 from VMA-513, sits amidst a variety of Navy, Marine, and Canadian aircraft at NAS Alameda, California, in October 1983. The installation of the formation strips on the vertical stabilizer obliterates part of the squadron tail code letter "F" and severs part of the bureau number. *(T. Chee)*

Two AV-8Cs from VMA-513 "WF" prepare to launch from the *Guadalcanal* in November 1983. Because it is impossible to communicate vocally during air operations, hand signals are used as well as message boards. The messages on the board can include estimated weight, trim, nozzle angle, vertical takeoff (VTO), standard takeoff (STO), or other pertinent information.

AV-8C BuNo.159247 from VMA-542 (WH) "Flying Tigers" is at rest on the Naval Air Facility (NAF) ramp in Washington, D.C., on a clear October day in 1984. VMA-542 was commissioned on 1 November 1972 and moved from MCAS Beaufort, South Carolina, to MCAS Cherry Point in June 1974 to become part of Marine Air Group (MAG)-20. *(D. F. Brown)*

Practice Multiple Bomb Rack

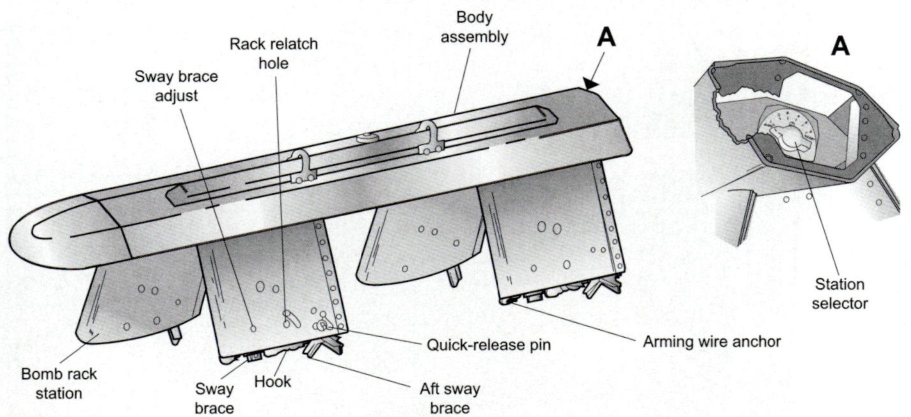

The A/A37 B-3 practice multiple bomb rack (PMBR) has six release assemblies. It is designed to carry one to six Mk 76 and/or Mk 106 practice bombs, or the Mk 58 marine location marker (MLM) that produces a long-burning smoke and flame reference point marking on the ocean's surface. The PMBR weighs 87 pounds, is 65 inches in length, and is 21 inches wide. *(Courtesy U.S. Marine Corps)*

Marine Harrier TAV-8A, TAV-8B

Marine Attack Training Squadron (VMAT)-203 "Hawks" was the only U.S. Marine squadron to operate the TAV-8A. The squadron received the first of eight two-seaters, BuNos.159378-159385, in late 1975. The TAV-8As served the squadron until 1987, when the remaining five were ferried to Davis-Monthan Air Force Base for storage at Aerospace Maintenance and Regeneration Center (AMARC). The Marine two-seaters, unlike the British two-seat Harriers, did not have the radar warning receiver system nor the laser ranger and marked target seeker. In addition, the American TAV-8A had only two pylons and was not combat capable, whereas the British two-seater has four pylons and can mount gun pods and weapons pods. The U.S. Marine TAV-8A had the larger definitive tail.

The original decision by the Marines to forgo the development of a dedicated trainer version of the AV-8B was thankfully reversed when it was realized that Harrier pilot trainees were experiencing their first flights in a TAV-8A, which was an all-analog 1960s cockpit. The pilot trainees were expected to solo in an AV-8B that had a digital cockpit. The differences between the AV-8A/C and the AV-8B in the operating environment and the handling characteristics were significant enough to warrant consideration of a dedicated trainer. It was three years between the introduction of the first VMAT-203 AV-8Bs and the welcome sight of a much-needed TAV-8B on the VMAT-203 flight line.

The first TAV-8B was the 65th Harrier II and made its first flight in the skilled hands of test pilot Bill Lowe on 21 October 1986. The TAV-8B has full dual controls, a taller fin with increased chord, and area for improved directional stability. The environmental control system is modified to cope with the demands of two cockpits.

The TAV-8B does not have the extended tail cone of the TAV-8A and has only two hard points for the main purpose of carrying fuel tanks, training weapons, or practice bombs. Twenty-four TAV-8Bs were ordered: 22 for VMAT-203 and two for the Italian Navy, BuNos.164136–164137. At least one TAV-8B, BuNo. 164137 modex (two-, three- or four-number code on the nose, tail, and wing flaps) 626, was assigned to the Naval Air Test Center at Naval Air Station (NAS) Patuxent River.

The CO's TAV-8B BuNo. 164141 is recognized by the two zeros on the nose, often referred to as "double nuts" in Navy and Marine parlance. The aircraft wears the current standard paint scheme of Dark Gray (FS 36118) on the top of the fuselage and inner parts of the wings and Gray (FS 36375) on the fuselage sides, outer periphery of the wings, tail, and the undersides.

This TAV-8A, BuNo. 159380 from VMAT-203, was the third production tandem-seat Harrier. It was also known as the Mk 54 in the United Kingdom. Red, white, and blue stripes bedeck the rudder. The F-95 square camera window is located in front of the port intake. This aircraft was written off on 12 August 1987.

TAV-8B BuNo. 163180 from VMAT-203 is having its engine checked. An upper panel aft of the cockpit area has been removed and placed on the deck in front of the four-wheeled ground support cart. When a major engine problem develops on a Harrier, it entails removing the entire wing from the aircraft.

Marine AV-8B Harrier II

By 1970, Engineers at Hawker Siddeley had already completed studies relevant to improvements for the Harrier. McDonnell Douglas Corp. (MCAIR) joined the project, and the Rolls-Royce Bristol team joined with Pratt & Whitney to develop a new Pegasus 15 engine. Most of the studies were done under the project numbers of P.1184 and P.1185. The project was commonly referred to as the Super Harrier.

The Pegasus 15 project resulted in an engine that produced 24,500 pounds of thrust. Engineers at Hawker and MCAIR were extremely satisfied at this point, since 25,000 pounds of thrust was the amount of thrust that engineers at Hawker and MCAIR were using in their studies to project the advanced performance of this new variant.

The RAF was not interested in this Harrier variant then due to budget constraints. But the U.S. Marine Corps was interested in a replacement for its A-4 Skyhawk, and an advanced Harrier would also fit nicely in the U.S. Navy's long-range plans to build a new class of versatile ships of 11,000 to 16,000 tons that would be capable of operating jet V/STOLs and helicopters in addition to other offensive systems.

This Super Harrier project, known as the AV-16A in the United States, was to be a V/STOL aircraft with a redesigned wing and tasked with carrying mission avionics and weapons specified by the U.S. Navy, U.S. Marine Corps, Royal Air Force, and Royal Navy. When the AV-16 studies were terminated by Hawker and MCAIR in 1975, both these companies pursued their own lines of development.

The major factor for the demise of the AV-16 was attributed to the project development cost of $1 billion. BAE and McDonnell Douglas used a new approach to show the U.S. Marine Corps that with a number of airframe changes, the payload radius of the AV-8A could be significantly increased without the need to develop a new engine.

The feature that is prominent in the AV-8B is the new wing with its graphite composite structure, a supercritical airfoil, and a greater area and span. The wing has large slotted flaps, fitted leading-edge root extensions that enhance the aircraft's turning rate, and lift improvement devices, positioned beneath the fuselage as well as on the gun pods, that reduce hot gas recirculation. The wing can accommodate 2,000 pounds more internal fuel than the AV-8A and is fitted with six hard points; the AV-8A had four. The cockpit is positioned approximately 10.5 inches higher than on the AV-8A, allowing additional space for avionics. The bubble canopy improves the pilot's view, the nose of the aircraft was enlarged to provide additional space

YAV-8B BuNo.158394 was one of two developmental aircraft rebuilt from the last two of the first lot of AV-8As. This photo shows the aircraft over one of the runways at the McDonnell Douglas aircraft plant. *(McDonnell Douglas)*

The third full-scale development aircraft, BuNo.161398, is painted in the three-color scheme of dark green, dark gray, and light gray. Unlike the first AV-8B, BuNo.161396, this aircraft had one leading edge fence on each wing. It also had the 100 percent LERX in place. The first four developmental aircraft had a redesigned intake with double rows of inlet suction intake relief doors. The main improvement over the AV-8A was a wing that had an area that was 14.5 percent greater, and a span that was increased by 20 percent. *(McDonnell Douglas)*

for avionics and other equipment, and the front windscreen was increased in size. It was a single curved piece of acrylic with deicing features. No wiper blade was needed.

The Harrier II cockpit is new. A lot of features are directly related to the F/A-18 program, such as the multifunction display (MFD). The up-front control (UFC) for communication/navigation/identification (CNI) incorporates a fiber-optic data converter. The Harrier II uses the GAU-12U gun. It has five 25 mm barrels and is mounted in the port pod on the underside of the fuselage, and 300 rounds of ammunition are stored in the starboard pod. Both pods are aerodynamically identical.

Two YAV-8Bs were built (BuNos. 158394 and 158395). Four full-scale development (FSD) AV-8Bs (BuNos. 161396–161399) were produced. The first batch of production AV-8Bs included BuNos. 161573–161584 (12), and the second batch included BuNos.162068–162085 (18). A total of 306 AV-8Bs were produced.

The first full-scale development aircraft, BuNo.161396, lifts off on a test flight in November 1981. The lift improvement devices (LIDs) — the enlarged strakes and retractable air dam located directly behind the nose gear — are quite visible. The aircraft does not have the leading edge root extension (LERX) installed, and it has two leading edge fences in place on both wings. *(McDonnell Douglas)*

AV-8B BuNo.162949 from the dedicated Harrier Training Unit VMAT-203 "Hawks" was photographed while on a training flight. It carries the tail code "KD," and its aircraft number is in white. This aircraft was upgraded to an AV-8B II Plus in fiscal year 1997 and assigned BuNo. 165356. *(D. Linn)*

An AV-8B II from Marine Medium Helicopter Squadron (HMM)-261 with the tail code "EM" lands aboard the *Saipan* (LHA 2) on 9 June 1990. The squadron was preparing for Operation Sharp Edge off the coast of Liberia. The Harrier is not carrying any ordnance or external fuel tanks. *(JO1 K. Burke)*

In 1988, VMA-331 "Bumble Bees" experimented with a new paint scheme for their AV-8Bs. This shot on the ramp at MCAS Cherry Point depicts Maj. Gen. R. A. Gustafson's personal aircraft, BuNo. 162069. The triple zeros identifies it as the "Boss Bird." The Dark Gray is FS 36118, and the Light Gray is FS 36375. *(D. Linn)*

AV-8B BuNo.163206 from VMA-542 with tail code "WH" made an appearance at the NAS Norfolk Open House in April 1992. The triangles on the rudder are yellow. This aircraft crashed on the Chocolate Mountain Gunnery Range near Yuma, Arizona, during training on 7 October 1996 while assigned to VMA-223. *(D. Linn)*

Marine AV-8B Harrier Night Attack (NA)

The Harrier AV-8B (NA) was originally referred to as the AV-8D. The retirement of the A-6E Intruder in April 1993 left the Marine Corps without a dedicated long-range all-weather heavy attack aircraft. McDonnell Douglas was awarded a $2.1 million design definition contract for the Night Attack Harrier in 1985.

The Night Attack Harrier received the new F402-RR-408 engine, which was developed from the XG-15 engine technology demonstration program that was jointly funded by the British Ministry of Defence and Rolls-Royce on a 70/30 percent basis. The new engine has improved fan aerodynamics, single crystal turbine blades, and a myriad of other improvements and modifications. Thrust end inspection cycle was doubled to 1,000 hours. Engine thrust was improved greatly, with Rolls-Royce claiming a short lift wet rating of 23,800 pounds and McDonnell Douglas claiming 24,500 pounds. (The U.S. Marine Corps rating was 23,400 pounds.) In addition, the new variant of the Harrier was fitted with four extra Goodyear Tracor AN/ALE-39 chaff/flare dispensers above the rear fuselage. This increased the number of flare or chaff cartridges to a total of 180, compared to the 60 that could be carried on the ventral AN/ALE-39 on the standard AV-8B.

The 87th single-seat AV-8B (BuNo.162966) was built as the first AV-8B (NA) prototype flying on 26 June 1987 at China Lake, California. The first production AV-8B (NA) BuNo.163853 was the 167th single-seater, the second fiscal year aircraft. In the fall of 1989, Marine front-line squadrons began transitioning to the AV-8B Night Attack (NA) Harrier II. VMA-214 was the first squadron to receive the Night Attack version of the Harrier in 1989. By 1992, all the Marine Harrier squadrons were flying Night Attack Harriers. Air Development Squadron (VX)-9 (previously VX-5) operated the Night Attack prototype BuNo. 162966, which crashed near NAS China Lake on 27 September 1994.

The most distinguishing feature on the AV-8B (NA) is the forward-looking infrared pod in front of the windscreen. In conjunction with the FLIR system, the pilot is provided with GEC Cat's Eyes Generation III night vision goggles with a field of view of 40 degrees in azimuth by 30 degrees. This gives better peripheral vision outside the 22-degree cone covered by the FLIR.

A VMA-211 AV-8B (NA), BuNo.163874, "Island Avengers" proudly displays its new paint scheme while at rest on the transit line at NAS Moffett Field, California, on 29 April 2000. All markings are in dark gray. The roundel with the star in the middle signifies the lineage of the squadron and its role in the defense of Wake Island in World War II. *(T. Chee)*

An AV-8B Harrier Night Attack (NA) assigned to Strike Directorate NAS Patuxent River for testing is buttoned up and being towed by a yellow tractor. Moving aircraft around by this means saves money and eliminates the possibility of an engine ingesting foreign object debris (FOD). The paint scheme is a wraparound dark green and dark gray.

This AV-8B (NA), BuNo.163868 from VMA-214 (WE) "Black Sheep," carries the dark green and dark gray wraparound scheme with all other markings in black. The outrigger wheel struts are white except for the moving parts that are stainless steel. The wheel hub and the interior of the outrigger wheel housing are also painted white *(D. F. Brown)*

AV-8B Night Attack System

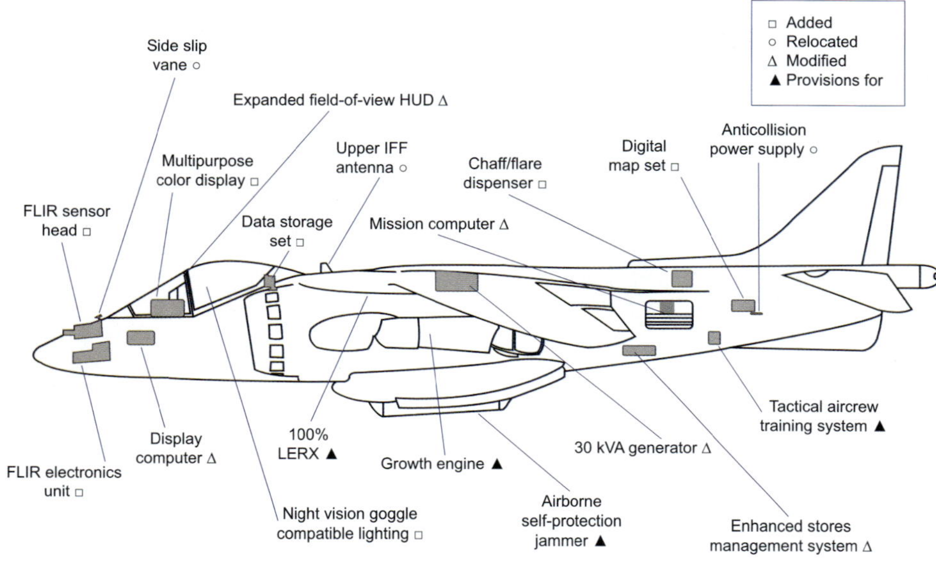

These two AV-8B (NA) Harriers from VMA-214 (WE) "Black Sheep" are being refueled. The purple-shirted fuel handler on the wing with the fuel hose in hand is assisted by a number of other members of the team, who are standing between and aft of the two aircraft. Plane handlers positioned forward of aircraft number 16 are wearing blue shirts. The aircraft remain secured to the deck. *(J. Z. Baddorf)*

Cat's Eyes Night Vision Goggles

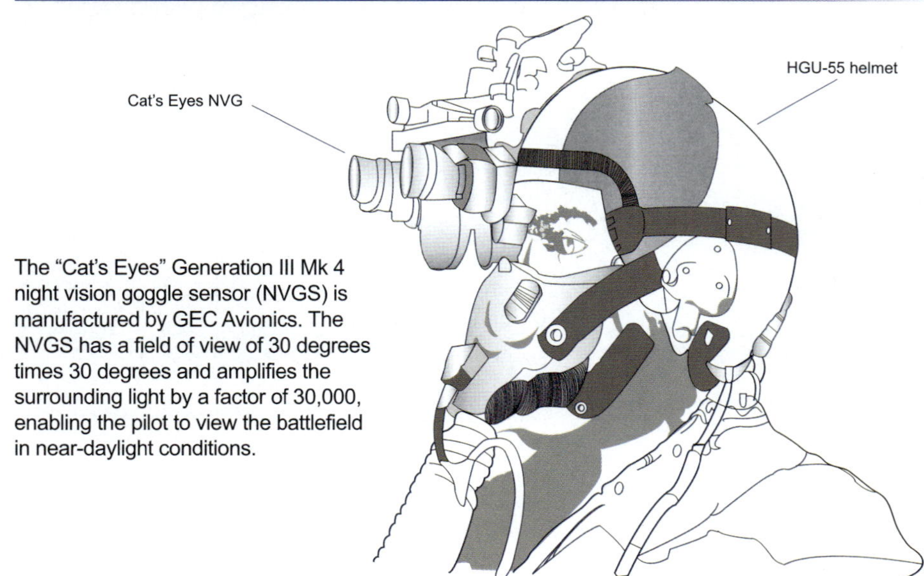

The "Cat's Eyes" Generation III Mk 4 night vision goggle sensor (NVGS) is manufactured by GEC Avionics. The NVGS has a field of view of 30 degrees times 30 degrees and amplifies the surrounding light by a factor of 30,000, enabling the pilot to view the battlefield in near-daylight conditions.

One of the first Marine Squadrons to receive the upgraded night attack system for the AV-8B II was VMA-513 "Flying Nightmares." The navigation forward-looking infrared sensor (NAVFLIR) was produced by GEC Avionics in the United Kingdom. This system provides the dual function of night navigation and target acquisition. *(K. Snyder)*

This AV-8B (NA) from VMA-311 is preparing to launch from the *Tarawa* (LHA 1) during Exercise Kernal Blitz in 2001.The aircraft is carrying 500-pound bombs on the middle pylon of each wing. VMA-311 received its first AV-8B II in May 1992. *(Sgt. C. Surber)*

A VMA-214 (WE) AV-8B (NA) recovers from a practice bombing run. Triple ejection racks are carried on the intermediate pylons. The double zeros on the nose indicate that this is the commanding officer's aircraft.

AV-8B II (NA) BuNo. 163865 from VMA-214 sits on the ramp at Lakefront Airport during the Cleveland National Air Show in September 1990. It is painted in the Dark Green (FS 34079) and Dark Gray (FS 36173) wraparound paint scheme. *(C. Mesker)*

A pristine AV-8B (NA) BuNo.164152 from VMA-211 "CF" made an appearance at the Oklahoma City Air Show in July 1994. The squadron received its night attack Harriers and AV-8B Pluses in the spring of 1990. (See its profile on page 26.) *(G. James)*

Marine AV-8B Harrier II Plus

In June 1987, British Aerospace and McDonnell Douglas made a joint announcement that they intended to develop a radar-equipped variant of the Harrier. The U.S. Marine Corps, Italian Navy, and Spanish Navy became seriously interested, and in September 1990 a tripartite Memorandum of Understanding among the nations of Italy, Great Britain, Spain, and the United States was signed to develop the current version of the Harrier known as the Harrier II Plus. The Italian company Alenia and the Spanish Company CASA each garnered 15 percent shares in the program.

A critical feature of the program was the adoption of the Hughes AN/APG-65 pulse-Doppler radar that closely resembles the radar that was being used in the FA-18 Hornets at the time. The scanner (24 by 28 inches) was redesigned because of the size of the nose cone. The software was also modified, and a new circuit card was provided for the target data processor. The thinking of the people at McDonnell Douglas was to develop an AV-8B that utilized the offensive and defensive features of the FA-18C, highly desirable since the USMC and Spanish Navy are operating FA-18s. Increased commonality between aircraft in service is a very cost-effective remedy to the ever-rising cost of maintaining a military force.

The Harrier II Plus was based on the Night Attack AV-8B and retained full night attack capability. Its FLIR fairing on the nose was more angular than that found on the AV-8B (NA). It had the 100 percent leading-edge root extensions, twin Goodyear Tracor AN/ALE-39 chaff/flare dispensers on each side of the upper rear fuselage, and a lengthened ram air intake at the forward base of the vertical stabilizer.

The U.S. Marines originally ordered 27 new-build Harrier II Pluses, but later increased this order to 31 new-build airframes. The new-build Harrier II Pluses were delivered to three front-line squadrons at MCAS Cherry Point. VMA-542 was the first squadron to received the new Harrier on 8 July 1993. VMA-223 received its Harriers in late 1993, and VMA-231 received its Harrier II Pluses in 1994. All Marine Harrier squadrons are currently flying AV-8B II (NA) or AV-8B II Pluses.

The Harrier II Plus is powered by the F402-RR-408 (Pegasus 11-61) engine, which delivers 23,800 pounds of thrust.

A heavy weather AV-8B II Plus from U.S. Navy Air Test and Evaluation Squadron (VX)-9 sits on the ramp at NAS China Lake in October 1997. VX-9 was formed by the merger of VX-4 and VX-5 on 30 September 1994. The squadron uses the tail code "XE" and wears the upside-down bat with two lightning bolts. VX-9 assumed the responsibility for the Initial Operational Test and Evaluation (IOT&E) of the AV-8B II Plus. *(M. Roth)*

The commanding officer of VMA-223 "Bulldogs" had the tail of his AV-8B II Plus BuNo. 165354 (WP) painted to show some of the aircraft that were flown by the squadron in the past. In late 1993, the "Bulldogs" was the second Harrier squadron to receive the AV-8B II Plus. VMA-223 was activated in May of 1942 during World War II.

An AV-8B II Plus prepares to launch on a night mission from Al Asad AB in Iraq in January 2005. A GBU-12 is carried on station three under the port wing, and a LITENING pod is carried on station five. Two external fuel tanks are attached to stations two and six. The bright lights on the wing tips are navigation lights. *(M. Steele)*

(Clockwise from upper left)
This AV-8B Harrier II Plus with VMA-223 prepares to land on the amphibious assault ship *Nassau* (LHA 4). This model of the Harrier is capable of night and adverse weather operations and is equipped with the Hughes AN/APG-65 pulse-Doppler radar. *(A. King)*

A brace of Harrier II Pluses prepare to refuel from a U.S. Air Force KC-10 Extender from the 380th Air Expeditionary Wing over Iraq on 3 October 2004. The top Harrier II Plus has a LITENING pod on the inboard starboard pylon and a GBU-12 on the port inboard pylon. *(Tech. Sgt. E. Gudmundson)*

Laser-guided bombs on a dolly are being moved into position to be mounted on a VMA-231 AV-8B II Plus. The tip of the LGB has a cap to protect the sensitive nose of the weapon. The forward section is painted olive drab, the two rings are yellow, and the aft section is a light gray color. *(PH3 J. Taucher)*

This VMA-3II AV-8B II Plus prepares to launch from the amphibious assault ship *Boxer* (LHD 4). *Boxer* was part of the *Kitty Hawk* (CV 63) Strike Group's third annual Joint Air And Sea Exercise (JASEX) 2005 with USAF and USMC forces in the Western Pacific. The Harrier is carrying 300-gallon external fuel tanks on stations two and six. *(PHAN P. Pollach)*

AV-8B Harrier II Plus

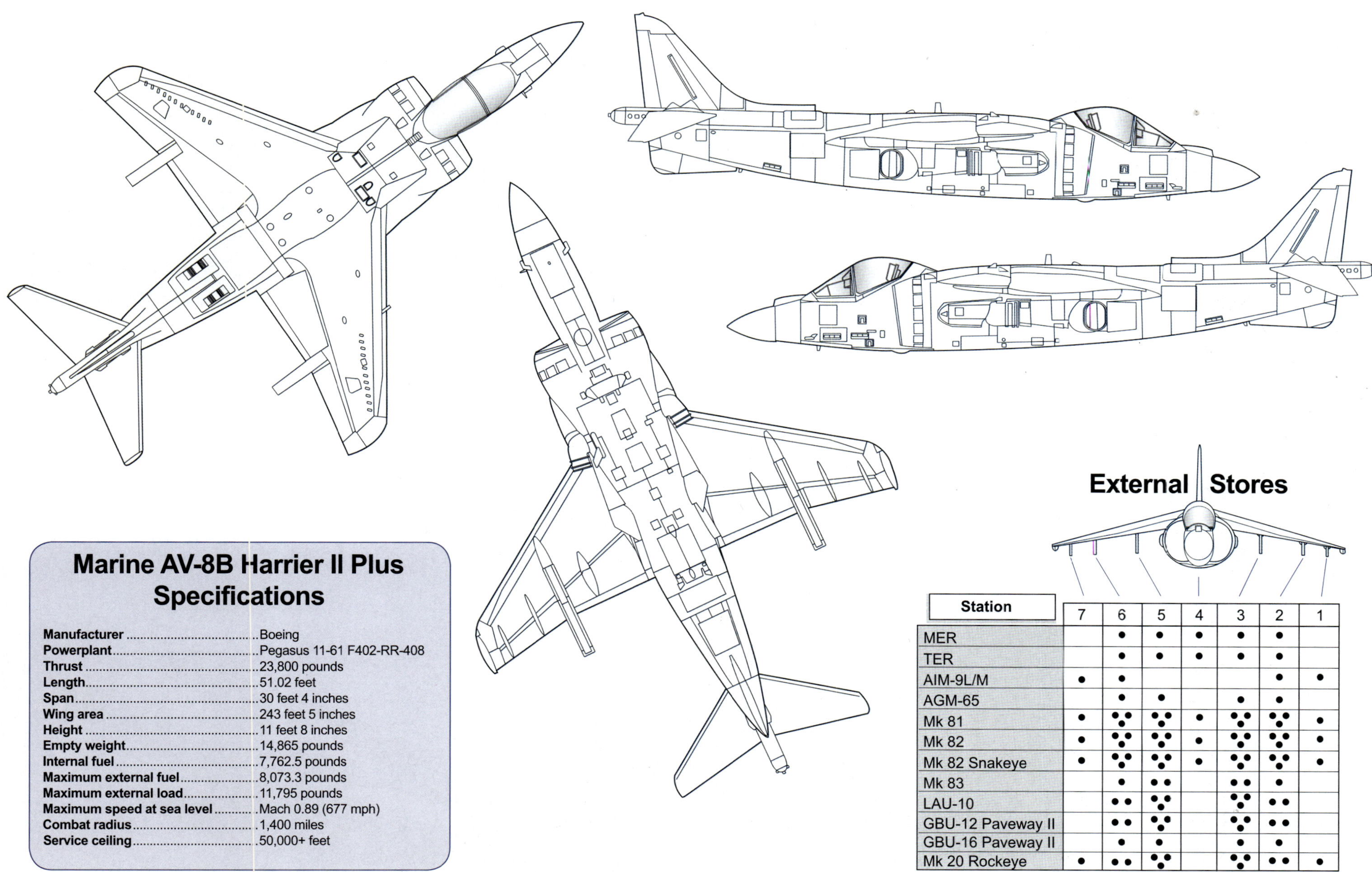

External Stores

Station	7	6	5	4	3	2	1
MER		●	●	●	●	●	
TER		●	●	●	●	●	
AIM-9L/M	●	●				●	●
AGM-65		●	●		●	●	
Mk 81	●	●●●	●●●	●	●●●	●●●	●
Mk 82	●	●●●	●●●	●	●●●	●●●	●
Mk 82 Snakeye	●	●●●	●●●	●	●●●	●●●	●
Mk 83		●	●●		●●	●	
LAU-10		●●	●●●		●●●	●●	
GBU-12 Paveway II		●●	●●●		●●●	●●	
GBU-16 Paveway II		●	●		●	●	
Mk 20 Rockeye	●	●●	●●●		●●●	●●	●

Marine AV-8B Harrier II Plus Specifications

Manufacturer .... Boeing
Powerplant .... Pegasus 11-61 F402-RR-408
Thrust .... 23,800 pounds
Length .... 51.02 feet
Span .... 30 feet 4 inches
Wing area .... 243 feet 5 inches
Height .... 11 feet 8 inches
Empty weight .... 14,865 pounds
Internal fuel .... 7,762.5 pounds
Maximum external fuel .... 8,073.3 pounds
Maximum external load .... 11,795 pounds
Maximum speed at sea level .... Mach 0.89 (677 mph)
Combat radius .... 1,400 miles
Service ceiling .... 50,000+ feet

A VMA-231 AV-8B II Plus commemorates the 80th anniversary of the squadron by painting the tail of the Harrier in a striking paint scheme. The inscription in white reads "Ace Of Spades Since 1919." VMA-231 is the oldest squadron in the U.S. Marine Corps. (See its profile on page 26.)

Engines are very susceptible to damage under adverse weather conditions, especially in an environment where sandstorms occur. The fine sand particles invade engine compartments, requiring constant attention. This AV-8B II Plus from VMA-223 based at Al Asad, Iraq, is having a new engine installed under the watchful eyes of power line personnel. *(Chief Warrant Officer-2 C. L. Beasley)*

This AV-8B II Plus, BuNo.165386, is being given the signal to launch from the launch officer, who is wearing a yellow vest. This identifies him as an individual responsible for the movement of aircraft on the deck. A 1,000-pound LGB is mounted on station six. The carrier is the *Bataan* (LHD 5) *(Lance Cpl. J. Ross)*

An AV-8B II Plus attached to HMM-262 at MCAS Futenma, Japan, does a practice landing at Ie Shima, Japan, on 27 April 2006. The pilot is landing on a painted runway that is painted like that found on a multipurpose amphibious assault ship, known as an LHD. There are presently seven LHDs in service, and one is under construction. *(Lance Cpl. Z. Griffin)*

A VMA-231 AV-8B II Plus lands aboard *Bataan* on 19 August 2006. The squadron was working with HMM-264, 26th Marine Expeditionary Unit (MEU). The two units are involved in Expeditionary Strike Group Integration (ESGI).

Two AV-8B II Plus Harriers attached to HMM-266 "Fighting Griffins" are being signaled by launch officers to prepare to launch. The lead aircraft is carrying two 300-gallon fuel tanks on the inboard pylons, and the rear Harrier has a LITENING pod on the starboard inboard pylon. The squadron carries the letters "ES" on the tail. The squadron is serving aboard *Wasp* (LHD 1) in the Indian Ocean in April 2004. *(PM3 T. Ellison)*

AV-8B Noses

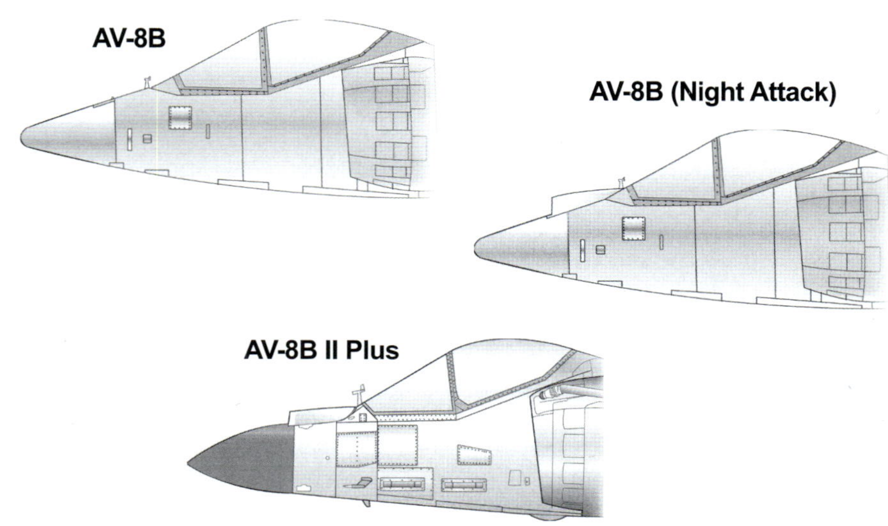

An AV-8B II Plus, under the watchful eye of the launch officer, lifts off the forward end of *Bataan*'s deck on 5 March 2003. Two 300-gallon tanks are positioned on stations two and six. When fuel tanks have to be jettisoned, it is done in pairs from stations two and six first, and then from stations three and five. The carrier is part of Amphibious Task Force East (ATF-E). *(J. D. Lee)*

This VMA-223 AV-8B II Plus aboard the *Nassau* has its engine turning. Still chained to the deck, tie-downs are not removed from aircraft until brake hydraulic pressure is confirmed by the pilot. A "start the engine" is given by the plane director.

These hard-working aviation boatswain's mates are positioning JP-5 fuel hoses in preparation to fuel AV-8B II Pluses from HMM-365 aboard *Bataan* during Operation Enduring Freedom on 11 January 2002. The tail code "YM" is assigned to this squadron. When Harriers are temporarily assigned to helicopter squadrons, they assume the tail code of the squadron but usually retain their original rudder squadron markings. *(PH3 J. Taucher)*

An AV-8B II Plus taxies at Al Asad Air Base in Iraq on 17 February 2007. The aircraft belongs to VMA-211 "CF" and is carrying an LAU C/A, which holds four 5-inch rockets on station three. The rockets can be fired in single or ripple mode. VMA-211 was the first Marine Harrier squadron to launch an all Joint Direct Attack Munition (JDAM) strike; it occurred on 9 November 2006. *(Sgt. A. Gaus)*

Indian Navy FRS.51

In 1983, the Indian Navy ordered six FRS.51 Sea Harriers and two T.60 two-seat Harriers that were to operate from the carrier INS *Vikrant*. The first three FRS.51s of No. 300 Indian NAS were delivered to their new base at Goa, India, in December 1983 after a ferry flight of 4,800 nautical miles from the United Kingdom.

The FRS.51s were basically FRS.1s as used by the British Navy. Some of the differences were that the Indian Sea Harriers used a gaseous oxygen system in place of liquid oxygen, had a modified radar system, and used Indian-specified radios. The aircraft were also wired for the French Matra Magic missile instead of the Sidewinder.

Ten more Sea Harriers were ordered in 1985 and delivered in the 1989–1991 timeframe. Another delivery of seven FRS.51s followed in late 1991 and 1992. This made a total of 23 FRS.51s that were in the Indian Navy inventory. No. 300 Squadron "White Tigers" currently has 15 FRS.51s and four T.60s in service.

The Sea Harriers are expected to be retired by the year 2010. The Indian Navy's T.60s that were modified from RAF surplus T.4s, ZB600 and ZB602, were procured in the 1990s as spares. Over the years, six T.60s were ordered by the Indian Navy.

The FRS.51s and T.60s operated from *Vikrant* until the carrier was scrapped. Presently the *Viraat* , which was refitted with a 12-degree ski jump in 1991, handles all carrier operations. This carrier is the former HMS *Hermes* that served the British Navy so well in the Falklands War.

(Above) The first FRS.51 made an appearance at the Farnborough International Air Show in September 1982. The British serial G-9-478 is still visible on the fuselage. The paint scheme is the standard British paint scheme at the time, gloss Extra Dark Sea Gray (BS381C:640) and white. IN 601 was delivered to the Indian Navy on 5 October 1984. It was written off in May 1988. *(L. Peacock)*

(Below) An over-the-wing view shows the positioning of the Indian roundel (saffron, white, and green) on the starboard wing. The roundel is carried on both the upper and lower wings, as well as on both sides of the fuselage just aft of the intakes. The 12 nubs on the forward part of the wing are vortex generators. *(S. Watson)*

An FRS.51 launches from its inland base at Indian Naval Air Squadron (INAS) Hansa. The new paint scheme is overall Medium Sea Gray (BS381C:637). The 100-gallon fuel tank has not been repainted, and is in the old standard paint scheme of dark sea gray and white. Crew training for INS 300 is the responsibility of INAS 551B "Braves." *(S. Watson)*

(Above) The port side of IN 808 was photographed at NAS Hansa in February 2005 wearing the colors that were initially applied to the first Indian Sea Harriers. Although the FRS.51s have been in service with the Indian Navy since 1984, the aircraft have been well maintained. This aircraft, formerly ZG942 when it served in the British Royal Navy, was delivered to the "White Tigers" of INAS 300 in Goa, India, in 1989. *(B. Archer)*

(Below) This FRS.51, IN 18 assigned to INAS 300 "White Tigers," is based at Hansa, the Indian Navy's principal airbase. Maintenance personnel are checking over the aircraft following a training mission. The aircraft is painted Dark Sea Gray (BS381C:638), with Barley Gray (BS4800.18B.21) undersides that quickly show dirt from the exhaust, which is emitted from the aft nozzles. The leaping tiger is positioned on both sides of the forward fuselage. *(S. Watson)*

(Above) A close-up of the tail on the INAS 551B T.60 shows the white tiger with black stripes with red front claws and a red tongue. The upside-down yellow "J" above the tiger's head designates an attachment point. The word "Navy" written in Hindi is black. The leading edge of the vertical stabilizer is black, and the rear warning radar is also visible. *(S. Watson)*

(Below) Chained to the deck, an FRS.51, IN 617, sits aboard the INS *Viraat* in February 2007 during operations in the Indian Ocean. Aircraft handlers are standing to port of the aircraft while it completes an engine run-up test. *(S. Watson)*

This INAS 551B squadron T.60 (black 651) in the dark sea gray/white undersides paint scheme is secured to the ramp by chains attached to the forward gear and the main gear. The ventral brake panel is in the deployed position. The white tiger is carried on both sides of the tail and forward fuselage. *(S. Watson)*

Aircraft handlers are preparing to move this FRS.51 to a new spot on the deck. Unlike U.S. Navy personnel who wear cranials to protect their skulls and hearing, the Indian Navy handlers in this photograph are wearing soft hats and yellow ear protectors. A white pod located on the starboard outboard pylon is a carrier bomb light store (CBLS), used to carry practice bombs. *(S. Watson)*

This T.60 with the laser nose from INAS 551B taxies out on a training mission. It is painted in the dark sea gray/barley gray paint scheme. The hulks of two aircraft are visible to the left of the aircraft. The white tiger is only featured on the starboard and port sides of the fuselage. *(S. Watson)*

A fly-over view of the *Viraat* shows three FRS.51 Sea Harriers. The one on the right is wearing the old paint scheme, and the other two wear the latest livery of overall Medium Sea Gray (BS381C:637). The numbered spotting circles on the deck are white. *(S. Watson)*

Italian Navy Harriers

The Italian Navy operates 16 AV-8B Harrier II Pluses and two TAV-8Bs. The order for the Harriers was placed in 1989. The first five single-seat and two-seaters were built by McDonnell Douglas in the United States; the remaining 13 were assembled at the Alenia factory in Italy.

The Italian TAV-8B is basically the same as the TAV-8B used by VMAT-203. It also has the larger vertical stabilizer, which is 1 foot 5 inches taller than the vertical stabilizer on the standard AV-8B Harrier II Plus. This tail enlargement was due to the change in the center of gravity as a direct result of the extension of the forward fuselage to accommodate the second seat. Unlike its British counterparts, it has only two hard points under each wing.

The Italian Navy received the TAV-8Bs in August 1991. Both the TAV-8Bs and the AV-8B Harrier II Pluses have the F402-RR-408 Pegasus 11-61 engine installed.

The Harriers are now operational with Primo Gruppo Aereo Marina Militare at Grottaglie, Italy. The Harriers operate from the CVS *Giuseppe Garibaldi*, a 10,000-ton ship that is about half the size of the Royal Navy's *Invincible*-class ships. Its air group can consist of 16 Harriers or 18 SH3D Sea Kings. It can also deploy with a combination of Harriers and Sea Kings.

(Clockwise from above)

An Italian AV-8B Plus lands aboard the *Giuseppe Garibaldi* (551) during Exercise Destined Glory in 2005. Two 300-gallon fuel tanks are carried on stations three and six. The Italian Harriers play an active role in NATO missions in Europe. *(PH1 Duckworth)*

This AV-8B Plus, matricola militare (mm) 7215 of Primo Gruppo Aereo, visited Grazzanise Air Base in Italy on 3 August 2002. A fake canopy has been painted on the underside to confuse enemy combatants in an air-to-air combat situation. The pilot's flight harness hangs on the middle starboard wing pylon. The inboard pylons hold 300-gallon fuel tanks that are painted semigloss black. *(S. Bottaro)*

One of two TAV-8Bs that were delivered to the Marina Militare Italia (MMI) in August 1991 sits parked at its new base at Grottaglie, located 12 miles from Taranto, Italy. A wolf's head adorns the starboard fuselage just aft of the white 01. Seven wolf paw prints are located on the rudder of (1-01) mm 55032. The two TAV-8Bs were originally assigned BuNos. 164136 and 164137 when they came off the production line in the United States, and both have the F402-RR-408 engine installed. *(I. Turniano)*

The display of six black bombs beneath the windscreen on this Primo Gruppo Aereo AV-8B II Plus mm 7224 indicates that this aircraft has been tested in battle. Its home base, Grottaglie, is near the naval base at Taranto in the southern coast area of Italy. *(I. Turniano)*

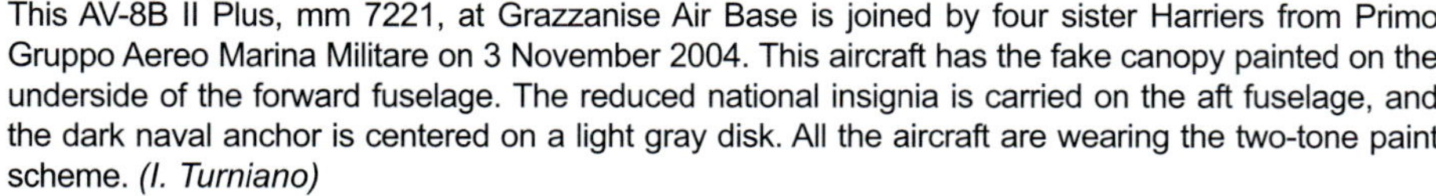

This AV-8B II Plus, mm 7221, at Grazzanise Air Base is joined by four sister Harriers from Primo Gruppo Aereo Marina Militare on 3 November 2004. This aircraft has the fake canopy painted on the underside of the forward fuselage. The reduced national insignia is carried on the aft fuselage, and the dark naval anchor is centered on a light gray disk. All the aircraft are wearing the two-tone paint scheme. *(I. Turniano)*

An Italian AV-8B II Plus (1-15) flies parallel to the Italian coastline with a Maverick AGM-65 missile located on the inboard pylon. The missile is painted a medium gray. An acquisition round is positioned on the outboard pylon. *(I. Turniano)*

An AV-8B II Plus (1-11), mm 7217, sits on the ramp at Practica on 28 May 2004. Positioned on the inboard port pylon is an inert GBU-12. The squadron known as the "Wolves" carries the wolf's head just below the windscreen, and has dark gray wolf paw prints painted on the rudder. *(I. Turniano)*

Spanish Navy Harriers

In 1973, the Spanish Navy ordered six Mk 53 and two Mk 54 Harriers from Hawker Siddeley Aviation Ltd. The American designation was AV-8S, and TAV-8S, respectively. In Spanish service, the single-seat Harrier was designated the VA-1, and the two-seater was the VAE-1. Both were called "Matadors."

In 1980, the Spanish naval air wing, known as the Arma Aerea de la Armada, purchased five more AV-8S Harriers, which were similar to the first batch. The first set of Harriers was shipped from the United Kingdom to the McDonnell Douglas Plant in St. Louis, Missouri, to be assembled. This was done to avoid a political uproar in the United Kingdom, since selling arms to the rightist government of Spain at the time would not have set well with the opposition parties. The second batch was supplied directly to Spain. BAE for its own reasons assigned a new designation of Mk 55 to the single-seaters.

The Spanish Harrier operates from land bases, primarily the naval base located at Rota, and the light carrier SNS *Dedalo*, which was the former jeep carrier USS *Cabot* (CVL 28). Since the *Dedalo* had a wooden deck, metal sheathing had to be laid down on the rear deck to allow Harrier landings.

When *Dedalo* was retired in 1988, it was replaced by the modern light carrier *Principe De Asturias*, which can accommodate eight Harriers and 14 helicopters. Beginning in 1987, the Spanish Harriers were fitted with the Marconi Sky Guardian rear warning radar. This was a highly sophisticated radar at the time and was capable of identifying the type of threat by comparing the radar signal with stored signatures of 200 aircraft.

In 1983, the Spanish Navy became the first export customer for the AV-8B Harrier II when it ordered 12 aircraft. The first three aircraft, designated EAV-8Bs with BuNos. 163010–163012, were delivered in October 1987. These Harriers became part of the new squadron identified as Escuadra 009. A total of 20 EAV-8Bs and a single TAV-8B were delivered to the Spanish Navy. Eight of the original 20 were ordered as AV-8B Harrier II Plus aircraft in March 1993; the remainder have been upgraded to the Plus configuration. The Spanish Navy replaced their AV8S Harriers and their two-seaters with the Harrier AV-8B IIs and TAV-8Bs beginning in late 1987. The surviving AV-8S and TAV-8S Harriers were sold to the Thai Royal Navy after being refurbished by the Spanish firm CASA prior to delivery.

A Harrier AV-8A(S), 008*12 from Escuadra 008, crashed at the Spanish Naval Base located at Rota, Spain, on 30 June 1986. The aircraft suffered an engine failure while it was hovering; the pilot ejected safely. Salvage workers are preparing to remove it from the site. *(PH2 D. Cummings)*

This AV-8A(S) visits Manises AB in France in April 1986. On the outboard pylon is the practice multiple bomb rack (PMBR) that is designed to carry small practice bombs. This aircraft is attached to Escuadra 008, home based in Rota, Spain. The scheme is Gloss Gull Gray (FS 16440) and white. The aircraft uses the Pegasus Mk 103 engine that produces 21,500 pounds of thrust. *(M. Fournier)*

A very attractive TAV.8A(S) from Escuadra 008 visited RAF Fairford in July 1994. This eye-catching aircraft has a stylistic shark's mouth in red and white and outlined in black. The tail is glossy black. This TAV-8A(S) was one of two TAV-8A(S) aircraft (T.2s), BuNos. 159563–159564, delivered to the Spanish Navy in 1976. (See its profile on page 27.)

An EAV-8B, 01-909 from Escuadra 009, in a very subdued two-tone gray color scheme, sits with its forward landing gear wheels chocked. The size of the Spanish roundel has been reduced as has the winged emblem of the Arma Aerea de la Armada on the tail. The word "ARMADA" is carried at the base of the vertical stabilizer on both sides and also on both sides of the forward fuselage.

Bearing a Maverick AGM-65 missile on station six, an EAV-8B Harrier II Plus (01-915) taxies after a practice mission. The missile is overall medium gray with two blue bands. The number 15 (black) is carried on the tail just below the small winged emblem of the Spanish Navy. *(T. Ziegenthaler)*

This EAV-8B II Plus (01-914) is chained to the deck of the carrier *Principe de Asturias* (R11) that was launched on 22 May 1982 and commissioned on 31 May 1987. *(E. Bannwarth)*

A TAV-8B taxies on the ramp at the large Spanish Naval Base, Rota, Spain. This tandem-seat Harrier (01-922) is the only one in the Spanish Navy and is assigned to 009 Escuadra. It carries the national roundels on the forward nozzle fairings and on the upper surface of the wings. *(T. Ziegenthaler)*

Royal Thai Navy Harriers AV8A, TAV-8A

When the Royal Thai Navy received the Spanish AV-8S Harriers in 1996, the Spanish name of "Matador" was dropped. The Royal Thai Navy uses the more common name "Harrier."

The Thais operate seven AV-8As and two TAV-8A two-seaters from land bases as well as from the light carrier RTNS *Chakri Naruebet*. Thailand's only carrier is designated as an offshore patrol helicopter carrier. The carrier, built by the Spanish shipbuilder IZAR, formerly E.N. Bazan, was delivered to Thailand on 4 August 1997. *Chakri Naruebet* is similar to the Spanish carrier *Principe De Asturias*, but shorter in length.

The ship's main role is surveillance, protection, and search and rescue. It can also serve as a flagship command and control vessel, air support for the Thai surface fleet, and disaster relief. She is based in the Gulf of Thailand.

The Royal Thai Navy's AV-8As and TAV-8As are based at U-Tapao with No. One Squadron and are now part of the First Air Wing. Originally, the designated squadron was number 301, and the wing number was Three.

Thai Navy pilots received their flight training at NAS Meridian, Mississippi, and NAS Kingsville, Texas, commencing in 1995. Following graduation from flight school, the pilots began extensive training on the AV-8S at the Spanish Naval Station in Rota, Spain, in 1996.

The package deal for the seven AV-8Ss and two TAV-8As cost the government of Thailand $70 million (U.S.) when the aircraft were purchased from Spain in 1992; they were delivered in 1997. Several USMC AV-8A/Cs were purchased from storage for spares.

(Above) This AV-8A is based at NAS U-Tapao, Thailand. It wears the colors associated with the U.S. Navy in the 1970s, glossy Light Gull Gray (FS 16440). The Harrier is assigned to the only Harrier Squadron in the Royal Thai Navy, No. One Squadron, First Air Wing. BuNo.161176 identifies it as one that was built originally for the Spanish Navy. (See its profile on page 25.) *(S. Bottaro)*

(Below) Two AV-8As are secured to the deck of HTMS *Chakri Naruebet*, the pride of the Royal Thai Navy's fleet. The crew is manning the rail as it heads to sea. The aircraft designation and bureau number is located on the bumper tail section of the fuselage. The nose color is the same as the fuselage color, but at present the noses are painted black. Some Royal Thai Harriers are now wearing a darker gray upper surface color. *(S. Watson)*

A Royal Thai Navy Harrier, 3104 BuNo.159557 from No. One Squadron, sits on the ramp at NAS U-Tapao on 7 January 1998. The Royal Thai Navy acquired seven single-seaters and a pair of TAV-8Ss from Spain in October 1996. The broad VHF band aerial in the center of the top side of the fuselage has been added for communication with helicopters at sea. *(S. Bottaro)*

F-35 Joint Strike Fighter

In November 1996, the Defense Department selected two major aerospace companies, Boeing and Lockheed Martin, to demonstrate two competing designs for the Joint Strike Fighter (JSF). On 26 October 2001, the Lockheed Martin team was selected to develop further and produce a family of conventional takeoff and landing (CTOL), carrier capable (CV), and short take-off vertical landing (STOVL) aircraft for the U.S. Air Force, Navy, and Marine Corps, and the British Royal Navy and other military allies.

The Joint Strike Fighter is expected to remain in production at least through the 2020s. It is planned to have the JSF manufactured in several locations. Lockheed Martin will build the aircraft's forward section in Fort Worth, Texas. Northrop Grumman will build the midsection in Palmdale, California, and the tail will be built by BAE Systems in the United Kingdom. Final assembly of the aforementioned components will take place in Fort Worth.

The plan is for the F-35 to be operated by a single pilot and have great survivability. It is to have all-weather strike capability that uses a wide variety of air-to-surface and air-to-air weapons, in conjunction with superior dogfight qualities. In addition, the increase in radius over present-day fighters will enable the pilot to operate with a limited dependence on air refueling, and have a greater amount of time on station to provide close air support (CAS) or combat air patrol. (CAP).

The F-35's mission systems were developed to give the pilot the advantage of being a tactician, thus increasing combat effectiveness. Next-generation sensors will provide the pilot with critical information from a number of onboard and off-board systems. The F-35 will have fighter-to-fighter data links as well as a satellite-communication capability for both transmitting and receiving.

A comparative analysis of the F-35 JSF Lightning II with the Harrier II Plus reveals the superiority of the JSF. The F-35 can go supersonic when needed and has an engine with 40,000 pounds of thrust. It has stealth features, low pilot workload, afterburner, internal and external weapons carriage, ability to conduct intensive operations for a sustained period, reliability to predict failures, and a true multirole capability.

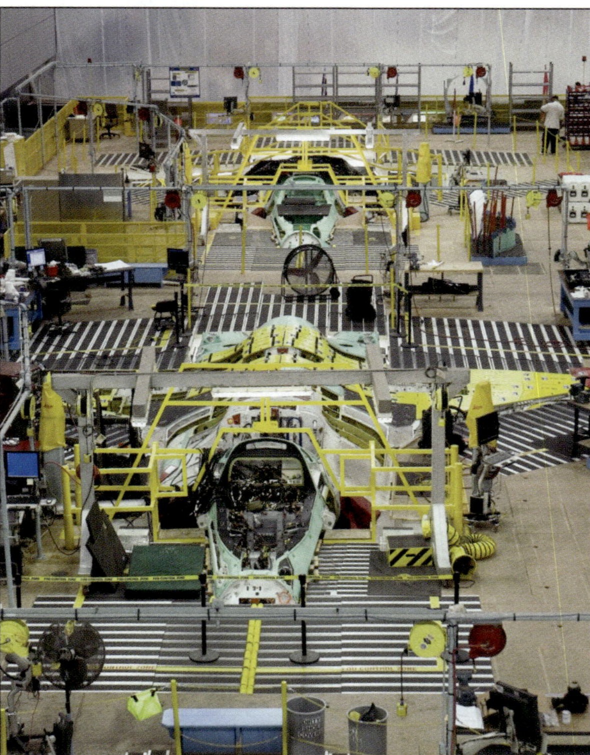

(Upper left)
The first two F-35B Lightning IIs sit in tandem on the assembly line of the Lockheed Martin facility located in Fort Worth, Texas. The yellow panels are conformal covers that protect the internal parts of the aircraft during assembly before the carbon fiber skins are attached. The Navy has built a $24 million facility for testing the F-35B and F-35C Lightning IIs. The first F-35B will arrive at NAS Patuxent River in early 2008. *(Lockheed Martin)*

(Upper right)
This Lockheed Martin X-35B is preparing to land vertically at Edwards AFB in California. The compass rose sits off to port on the desert floor. The X-35B was the first aircraft to have executed a short takeoff, level supersonic dash and vertical landing in the same flight. The first "Mission X" was piloted by Marine Maj. Art Tomassetti. *(Lockheed Martin)*

(Left)
In June 2001, the X-35B performed a series of vertical takeoffs and landings for the press at the Lockheed Martin's Palmdale, California, site. The pilots for the X-35B program were Simon Hargreaves of BAE Systems, Maj. Art "Turbo" Tomassetti, and RAF Squadron Leader Justin Paines. *(Lockheed Martin)*

The F-35B is a large aircraft. It is 51.1 feet in length and has a span of 35 feet. Each aircraft costs approximately $110 million. It will carry two 1,000-pound Joint Direct Attack Munition (JDAM) guided bombs and two advanced medium-range air-to-air missiles (AMRAAMs). A Gatling 25 mm cannon can be mounted on the centerline of the aircraft. The F-35B can land vertically, but it needs about 300 feet of runway to take off. When it begins its takeoff roll, the main engine is parallel to the runway. When the aircraft reaches a speed of 80 knots, the engine nozzle and lift-fan exhausts swing to a position perpendicular to the runway. This provides the vertical lift to get the aircraft in the air. (Lockheed Martin)